JUVENILE DELINQUENCY
Little Brother Grows Up

Volume 2
SAGE RESEARCH PROGRESS SERIES IN CRIMINOLOGY

ABOUT THIS SERIES

The *Sage Research Progress Series in Criminology* is intended for those professionals and students in the fields of criminology, criminal justice, and law who are interested in the nature of current research in their fields. Each volume in the series—four to six new titles will be published in each calendar year—focuses on a theme of current and enduring concern; and each volume contains a selection of previously unpublished essays . . . drawing upon presentations made at the previous year's Annual Meeting of the American Society of Criminology.

The *Series* begins in 1977 with four volumes, selected from papers delivered at the 28th Annual Meeting of the American Society of Criminology held in Tucson, Arizona, on November 4-7, 1976. The volumes in this inaugural year include:

- *Theory in Criminology: Contemporary Views,*
  edited by Robert F. Meier

- *Juvenile Delinquency: Little Brother Grows Up,*
  edited by Theodore N. Ferdinand

- *Contemporary Corrections: Social Control and Conflict,*
  edited by C. Ronald Huff

- *Criminal Justice Planning and Development,*
  edited by Alvin W. Cohn

We are pleased that these initial volumes in the *Sage Research Progress Series in Criminology* so well represent significant interdisciplinary contributions to the literature on criminology, juvenile delinquency, criminal justice administration, legal and ethical issues, and related areas. Comments and suggestions from our readers will be welcomed.

SERIES EDITORS:

James A. Inciardi
University of Delaware
Newark, Delaware

Gilbert Geis
University of California
Irvine, California

June 1977

SAGE RESEARCH PROGRESS SERIES IN CRIMINOLOGY
VOLUME 2

JUVENILE DELINQUENCY
Little Brother Grows Up

Edited by

Theodore N. Ferdinand

Published in cooperation with the
AMERICAN SOCIETY of CRIMINOLOGY

 **SAGE** Publications   Beverly Hills   London

For information address:

SAGE PUBLICATIONS, INC.
275 South Beverly Drive
Beverly Hills, California 90212

SAGE PUBLICATIONS LTD
28 Banner Street
London EC1Y 8QE

Printed in the United States of America

International Standard Book Number 0-8039-0916-0 (cloth)
International Standard Book Number 0-8039-0911-X (paper)
Library of Congress Catalog Card No. 77-81152

FIRST PRINTING

CONTENTS

Theodore N. Ferdinand
Northern Illinois University

1

INTRODUCTION

The study of juvenile delinquency has come a long way since the first juvenile court was established in Chicago in 1899. In the beginning the pioneering work of such scholars as Frederic Thrasher, Henry Shaw, David McKay, W.I. Thomas, Frank Tannenbaum, and William Healy was peripheral, not only to their parent disciplines of sociology and psychiatry, but also to the study of criminology itself. Many of the early criminologists, e.g., Sutherland or Bonger, were involved in much more epochal investigations and took little note of the achievements of their colleagues in delinquency research. As in the law, delinquency was handled differently by a different corps of workers than were adult criminals. The study of criminality was typically reserved to members of law faculties—especially in Europe—and by the time delinquency research began to gather momentum in the 1930s and 1940s, criminology was already an established discipline.

In 1955, however, the study of delinquency began to develop very rapidly and by the late 1960s not only were theories of delinquency assuming a high degree of sophistication, but attention was also increasingly drawn to the juvenile justice system. Albert Cohen's *Delinquent Boys* seemed to coalesce the vague concerns of scholars in social science, and in quick succession Cloward and Ohlin's *Delinquency and Opportunity*

[7]

and Matza's *Delinquency and Drift* appeared. Soon Walter Reckless and his students were publishing the results of their research into "good boys" in bad areas, and James F. Short, Jr., began his far-reaching research into the delinquent gangs of Chicago. About this time Walter Miller undertook to evaluate detached workers in Boston, and in the late 1960s Malcolm Klein did the same in Los Angeles. Finally, Travis Hirschi, utilizing a sophisticated research design and a sample of 4,077 juveniles from the Richmond, California, schools, sought to determine whether control theory, strain theory, or cultural deviance were adequate explanations of delinquency. Whatever else one may say of his research, the fact remains that it marked a high water mark in social science both in the sophistication of its theory and in the intricacy of its design. The 15 years following Albert Cohen's initial attempt to conceptualize the nature of delinquency was, indeed, a golden age in social science research.

Starting somewhat later the study of juvenile justice began also to attract attention. In 1963 Nathan Goldman completed his study of the juvenile in the hands of the police and the courts, and before long a whole host of studies of juvenile justice was under way. Landmark studies, however, were not so prominent here—rather a skein of smaller studies cumulated to pinpoint the problem areas of juvenile justice. Perhaps more important than scholarly research in this early period were two events in 1967—the *In Re Gault* ruling of the Supreme Court and the publication of the *Task Force Report: Juvenile Delinquency and Youth Crime* by the President's Commission on Law Enforcement and Administration of Justice. The former transformed the juvenile court by extending several due process protections to juveniles and the latter provoked wide discussion and concern in its descriptions of the breakdown in procedures used in handling juveniles both in court and in institutions. Together they forced scholars and practitioners alike to rethink their notions regarding the proper way to deal with delinquents in courts and in training schools.

The progress achieved in the 1950s and 1960s was impressive both in researching the sources of delinquency and in examining the procedures used to treat delinquents in the juvenile justice system. For a time in the late 1960s it is no exaggeration to suggest that the parent discipline, criminology, was eclipsed by the achievements of its younger offshoot, the study of delinquency. It is not idle boasting to assert that today "little brother" has, indeed, grown up.

Nevertheless, some of the momentum of the 1960s has subsided. The fury of the Vietnam War, the urban riots, and university rebellions seemed to press our attention to more urgent matters, and in the aftermath LEAA began to divert more and more resources into the study of crime and criminal justice. As a consequence, the only major theoretical innovation recently in delinquency research has been labelling theory, and the dominant goal of juvenile justice seems to be to divert juveniles from its harmful grasp.

The seven studies reported here accurately reflect these several themes in delinquency research. Three distinct concerns can be readily traced in the seven papers. First, four of the papers focus upon the impact of the courts and the police upon juveniles. Dungworth examined the dispositions of juveniles in a Michigan juvenile court and found that status offenders were handled differently than both felony offenders and misde meanants. His results are particularly interesting in that they seem to clear up some of the confusion surrounding similar studies in the past. Several studies have found that the juvenile's social background is more closely related to his disposition by the court than to his offense or offense history. Others have found just the opposite: that the juvenile's disposition depended more heavily upon his offense and his offense history than his social background (see Dungworth's paper for specific references).

Dungworth suggests that this apparent contradiction is not one at all. If status offenses and felony or misdemeanor offenses are handled differently by the courts, different studies focusing on different facets of the court's docket will certainly produce contrasting results. Dungworth's results also throw some light on the differential treatment accorded boys and girls, and whites and blacks—but readers will have to go directly to Dungworth's article for the details.

The only deficiency in Dungworth's study is the fact that he used the decision to detain the juvenile immediately following arrest as his dependent variable, rather than the ultimate disposition given the juvenile after his hearing. Undoubtedly, Dungwoth or someone else will extend his analysis to the more basic criterion and thereby pin this question down in a definitive way.

Dungworth's study was based upon a court in a relatively rural county—Calhoun—in a cosmopolitan state—Michigan. McDonald, Thilmony, and Schriner based their study upon a juvenile court in a relatively rural county in a decidedly rural state—North Dakota. Interestingly enough, however, their results imply that the turbulence of the late 1960s engulfed, if somewhat belatedly, many rural adolescents in this distinctly rural state.

One of the more interesting results of this research is the fact that the relationship between offense and disposition for first offenders shifts in 1970 from a positive to a negative one, i.e., the more severe the offense, the more severe the disposition, until 1970 when the relationship reverses. As the authors note, the 1970s witnessed an upsurge in female delinquency, and they note as well that girls tend to receive more severe dispositions than boys. Putting these two facts together, it is reasonable to suppose that the shift in relationship noted above reflects an increasing proportion of females in the delinquent population in the 1970s. It would be useful in this regard to distinguish between felony, misdemeanor, and status offenders, because, as noted in Dungworth's study, girls and boys are handled differently at all three levels—though not in a consistent fashion. Girls are given more severe dispositions for status offenses, but more lenient dispositions for felony and misdemeanor offenses. It may be that some of the mystery surrounding the reversal of the relationship between severity of offense and disposition would thereby be dispelled.

Even though much of the upsurge in delinquency in the 1970s reflected an increase in criminal referrals (cf. McDonald, Thilmony, and Schriner) the fact remains that 51% of the female referrals to this court in the 1970s committed status offenses. An increasing proportion of girl delinquents, there-fore, means a sharply increasing proportion of status offenders. And as Dungworth established, status offenders (and more particularly female status offenders) tend to receive more severe dispositions than felony offenders. The shifts in relationships noted in this paper may well reflect shifts in the mix of female and male delinquents along with shifts in the mix of felony, misdemeanor, and status offenders.

Datesman and Scarpitti continue the investigation into the effects of sex upon juvenile dispositions, but they extend it to include the impact of race as well. Their results are noteworthy. As with the previous studies, they report a clear relationship between sex and disposition. Girl delinquents are treated more leniently than boy delinquents for felony and misdemeanors, but more harshly for status offenses.

When Datesman and Scarpitti consider this relationship with race as an additional variable, they discover some interesting findings. They report, for example, much sharper differences in disposition between white boys and girls than between black boys and girls. Although they indicate that this difference holds for felons as well as misdemeanants, my reading of their data suggests that the difference is sharpest for misdemeanants.

Table 1 reveals that race has little to do with the disposition of *felony* offenders in juvenile court, but that it has a sharp effect upon both misdemeanants and status offenders. Black misdemeanants and particularly black female misdemeanants are given more severe dispositions than their white counterparts, and the same is true for white male status offenders. Datesman and Scarpitti explain these differences by suggesting that lower class black females tend to follow a more aggressive, more masculine role than their white counterparts. Hence, the difference between the sexes among black adolescents is less than that between white adolescents where the sex roles are more sharply differentiated. But if that were true, we would also expect black males and females to receive more similar dispositions for felony offenses as well. If black females are behaving generally more like males, they should commit more serious felonies than white females and receive more severe dispositions, which they do not.

Table 1: THE DISPOSITION OF JUVENILES ACCORDING TO OFFENSE, SEX, AND RACE[a]

	Felony Offenders				Misdemeanants				Status Offenders			
	Black		White		Black		White		Black		White	
Disposition[b]	Male	Female	Male	Female	Male	Female	Male	Female	Male	Female	Male	Female
Mild	44.7%	82.6%	45.1%	81.8%	64.8%	66.7%	76.4%	88.5%	61.8%	19.5%	32.5%	19.1%
Harsh	55.3	17.4	54.9	18.2	35.2	33.3	23.6	11.5	38.2	80.5	67.5	80.1

a. The computations for this table are based upon data presented in Susan K. Datesman and Frank R. Scarpitti, "Unequal Protection for Males and Females in the Juvenile Court," Table 4, in this volume.

b. A mild disposition is defined as one of the following: dismissed, warned, fined, or unsupervised probation. A harsh dispostion is defined as formal probation or assignment to a public institution.

Another explanation might take the following form. We have already seen that felony offenders tend to be judged primarily in terms of their offense and offense history. The absence of any substantial difference between the dispositions of black and white felony offenders probably reflects this fact. We also have seen that social background plays an increasingly important part in the dispositions of misdemeanants and status offenders, particularly for girls. The relatively high level of harsh dispositions for black misdemeanants and particularly for black female misdemeanants may reflect this fact, although this explanation, of course, could not explain why white male status offenders are treated so harshly by the juvenile court. It could be as Datesman and Scarpitti suggest, that juvenile judges where this research was undertaken do not evaluate black male status offenders in the same way they do whites and females. A disorganized social background for black male status offenders may not be viewed as negatively as the same kind of background for a female or a white adolescent. Datesman and Scarpitti suggest that those who deviate most from the standard applied by the judge should receive the most severe disposition, and the fact that white female status offenders who repeat their offenses receive the most severe dispositions tends to bear out their hypothesis.

Datesman and Scarpitti, however, are clearly impatient with the double standard applied by the court to males and females. They feel that it is based upon an outmoded view of femininity which holds essentially that the young girl must be protected from the temptations and corrupting influences of the community, when the family itself is ineffective in this regard. It is difficult to look into the minds of juvenile judges and conclude definitely that simple prejudice is the ruling factor. The fact remains, however, that an unwanted pregnancy contains many more implications for the welfare of young girls than it does for young boys, and it would be irresponsible for judges and others to suggest differently.

It is undoubtedly true that the double standard, which Datesman and Scarpitti criticize, is based upon the judge's desire to protect girls whose families are ineffective and who seem in danger of getting involved in situations from which they cannot easily be extricated. The double standard, of which we see ample evidence in these studies, may represent merely a desire on the part of the judge to prevent a difficult family situation from being compounded into a personal tragedy.

It is true that the double standard collides head-on with the Fourteenth Amendment of the Constitution, and it is equally true that placing a child on probation or in an institution is not always a good solution to a disorganized and destructive family situation. But to suggest that the judge faces a dilemma is not to suggest that there is an easy solution. To imply that the judge's duty is clear seems to me contrary to the facts.

The final paper in this series considers the origins of adolescent attitudes toward the police. Winfree and Griffiths have sampled high school students in five major cities to determine how they form their opinions of the police. Although they omit several pieces of information that would be interesting, they do provide us some insight into the ways in which adolescents form their impressions of the police.

I wish, for example, that they had included some indication of the relative level of support for the police among these high school students. Conventional wisdom has it that adolescent attitudes toward the police were rather unfavorable during the late 1960s and early 1970s, whereas today they are softening somewhat. Winfree and Griffiths went to great lengths to get a representative sample of American high school students, but they present no information regarding the level of approval or disapproval in their sample. Moreover, many of us with teenaged children are keenly aware of the fact that high school students are profoundly influenced in much of their thinking by their friends. This general fact, no doubt, extends to their attitudes toward the police and, therefore, it would have been interesting had Winfree and Griffiths gathered information on the status of their high school students among their peers to determine whether a central position or peripheral position affected how they felt about the police. The large amount of unexplained variance in attitudes toward the police in their path diagrams may reflect to some extent the impact of unmeasured peer influence.

Nevertheless, Winfree and Griffiths do point out that negative contacts with the police are nearly twice as important as positive contacts in determining adolescent attitudes toward the police. Many negative encounters involve direct personal confrontations with police officers, while many positive contacts represent rather distant, impersonal contacts. The importance of the former in shaping attitudes toward the police is quite reasonable when viewed in this light.

A second theme developed in these papers is the thesis, first advanced by Sykes and Matza in their classic article, "Techniques of Neutralization," in 1957 and expanded by Matza in *Delinquency and Drift* in 1964, that delinquents neutralize any lingering commitment they may have to conventional values and behavior by a variety of rationalizations or techniques of neutralization. Fritz Redl and David Wineman had suggested much the same in 1951 in *Children Who Hate,* but they had described it as a psychological mechanism, i.e., a "strategy of tax evasion." Few sociologically oriented authors took note of it. In any case, Matza proposed that delinquents are committed to both conventional culture and delinquent values and that techniques of neutralization nullify the former and enable the delinquent to behave in an antisocial manner without severe anxiety or inhibition.

Drawing upon attribution theory in social psychology, Ball suggests that neutralization is not so important as "attributed" neutralization, i.e., neutralizing attitudes attributed to the delinquent's peers, in releasing the juvenile from the inhibiting pressure of his conventional beliefs. Moreover, Ball indicates that attributed neutralization is primarily effective with boys and not girls. This latter finding deserves more study, for as Ball points out, it may be that neutralization is effective with girls but vis-à-vis a different set of behaviors. It may be that girls do relax their inhibitions regarding sexual behavior in response to attributed neutralization among their peers but that their inhibitions regarding parental defiance and the other measures of delinquency used by Ball are so strong that attributed neutralization has little effect upon them.

Austin approaches this same question, i.e., the relationship between neutralization and delinquency, but from a slightly different viewpoint. He suggests that both a commitment to delinquent values and neutralization are facets of the same thing—an acculturation to delinquent subculture. Austin questions Matza's assertion that delinquents are ambivalent about conventional life and that they belong more to a subculture of delinquency than a delinquent subculture. Austin's findings suggest that neutralizing beliefs are a part of the delinquent subculture and that the closer a juvenile approaches a delinquent subculture the more likely he is to endorse neutralizing attitudes among other things.

Both articles are important because they illuminate the social psychology of the delinquent, and they do so in the context of a reasonable, sophisticated theory of delinquent behavior. It is *only* through such painstaking efforts that the persuasive insights of the several theorists mentioned in the opening paragraphs of this introduction can be adequately specified and validated. There are many spokesmen today who denounce the scientific method as inappropriate to the advancement of human knowledge. Paradigms are relatively immune to the ebb and flow of empirical evidence, they assert. Whether this proposition is generally true cannot be debated here, but it is evident that Matza's thesis has been successfully challenged by the two authors appearing here.

The final theme to be explored in these papers is the popular belief today that juvenile institutions are ill suited to care for young people and should be closed down. The foremost spokesman for this point of view is, perhaps, Jerome Miller, who successfully closed all the juvenile institutions in Massachusetts in 1972. He is now the Governor's Special Assistant for Community Programs in Pennsylvania, and in 1975 Miller sought to divert delinquents from Camp Hill—an adult institution where juveniles were also housed—to community-based programs. Sprowls and Bullington examine the difficulties that awaited Dr. Miller as he set about to deinstitutionalize the care of delinquents in Pennsylvania. It is curious that the obstacles to deinstitutionalization in Pennsylvania were somewhat different than those Miller encountered in Massachusetts.

In Massachusetts, Miller's plan to close juvenile institutions was strongly opposed by correctional groups who were immediately threatened by it. In Pennsylvania, the staff at Camp Hill favored removing the juveniles because it would simplify somewhat their responsibilities. There remained sufficient adults at Camp Hill to keep the existing staff fully occupied. The difficulties in Pennsylvania consisted for the most part of arranging alternative programs for the displaced juveniles in the community. As in Massachusetts, these programs had to be painstakingly cultivated and carefully nurtured lest they founder and, as a result, deinstitutionalization took much longer than anyone had anticipated.

Sprowls and Bullington took advantage of their access to the records at Camp Hill to examine the committal and release policies utilized by the judges who sent juveniles to the institution, and their findings raise some interesting questions. They document, for example, that the several juvenile judges in the state use Camp Hill for quite different purposes and that racial prejudice may have been a factor in the terms served by black youths from certain counties. The latter finding is particularly interesting in view of other studies which report that race has a very slight influence upon disposition in the juvenile court. Dungworth, for example, reports here that the decision to detain juveniles who have committed felony offenses is virtually unaffected by race.

But Dungworth was looking at the decision to detain a juvenile immediately after arrest, and Sprowls and Bullington are looking at the term served by felony offenders in an institution. Many more people are involved in the latter decision, and it is entirely possible prejudice among correctional and court staff is cumulative and produces thereby much sharper discrepancies than with the simple decision to detain a juvenile following arrest. The Sprowls and Bullington paper suggests, therefore, that we need studies at every step in the disposition of juveniles. When such studies have been completed, we will have a much clearer picture of what factors affect the decision-making process at each step in the juvenile justice system, and we will be in a much better position to judge whether and how racial or sexual characteristics affect the individuals fate before the court.

Terence Dungworth
Michigan State University

2

DISCRETION IN THE JUVENILE JUSTICE SYSTEM
The Impact of Case Characteristics on Prehearing Detention

Juvenile court personnel are faced on a daily basis with the necessity for making decisions concerning intake, treatment, and disposition of the cases which are referred to them. In the majority of situations, however, clearly stated legal guidelines do not exist and, consequently, judges, referees, and administrators have great discretionary power. Most of them will admit and even stress the need for objective bases of decision making in the three areas, but few will argue that existing bases are satisfactory. The factors which are relevant to these decisions —including, for instance, the causes and attributes of delinquency and the impact of different types of action by the court—are numerous and poorly understood. This combination of complexity and inadequate theoretical specification leads to a situation where many if not most decisions are made by what seem to be intuitive or "seat of the pants" processes. To say this

AUTHOR'S NOTE: This paper is part of a larger study, begun in 1975 and continuing at present. I have been assisted in its development in a number of ways. I particularly want to thank Roger Lilkell, Administrator of the Calhoun County Juvenile Court. His openness, cooperation, and advice have been critical elements in whatever progress the project has made. I am also indebted to the College of Social Science at Michigan State University for financial assistance in the data collection and analysis stages. Finally, I want to thank Angela Horstman, who produced the manuscript effectively and with good humor, under conditions of some stress.

is not to criticize agency personnel, for the fact is that many decisions appear to turn out well, and, in any case, who among us could do better given these conditions? It does imply, however, that systematic research into the correlates of these decisions might shed light upon their determinants and might also suggest either salient objective criteria or avenues for future research to determine those criteria.

Because comprehensive analysis of the decision making in an organization is a large scale undertaking, I shall, for the purposes of this paper, focus upon the prehearing detention decision. The scope of the inquiry will be further narrowed to the empirical relationship between case characteristics and the detention decision. I shall not, therefore, attempt to consider legal, philosophical, or normative considerations concerning the decision, though, of course, these are proper and important areas of inquiry.[1] My objective is to assess the quantitative impact of case characteristics on the detention decision.

THE LOCUS OF THE RESEARCH

The data base for this study is drawn from the 1975 caseload of the Calhoun County Juvenile Court in Michigan. The court is based in Marshall, 35 miles south of Lansing, Michigan's capital city. Calhoun County is representative of much of Michigan and of the Midwest, in that it is comprised of several medium sized towns with some industry, along with substantial farming activities.

In 1975, the court handled 2,200 referrals of 1,607 juveniles. It is court practice to establish a case file at the time of referral and to update this file whenever subsequent referrals are made. The volume of information developed varies from case to case, depending primarily upon the degree of involvement with the court. If the referral is refused, for instance, or dismissed at an early stage, then the file characteristically contains personal identifiers—such as name, age, sex, race—and also the nature of the referral, but very little else. If the referral is accepted, however, a background investigation is conducted, and information is developed about the home and school environment of the case as well as these other data.

The court has made available the complete 1975 caseload, subject to privacy and security considerations consistent with LEAA guidelines, and for the purposes of this particular paper all cases, for which a prehearing detention decision was required, were retained.

The philosophy of the court with respect to detention is a humane one. Incarceration is not considered to be an automatic consequence of particular types of offense or home situations, but is a decision that is made on an individual basis in the light of the best evidence available. On occasion, of course, information is very limited. When, for instance, a police referral is made to the juvenile home at 3:00 a.m., the director of the home must make a virtually instant decision whether to accept or reject the case. However, this is the exception rather than the rule. At the present time, the court is in the process of establishing clearer guidelines for decision making, and anticipates that the findings of this research, among others, will assist in that process.

PRIOR RESEARCH

Previous research into this particular question has been somewhat limited, due, probably, to a number of inhibiting factors. First, the establishment and maintenance of data files of the kind of information needed to assess the relationship between case characteristics and court decision making is expensive and time consuming, and many courts lack the necessary financing and personnel. Second, even when such files exist, they are frequently not available to researchers, either because of privacy and security restrictions or because the resources needed to code and process the data are not forthcoming. Third, the generalizability of such inquiry is problematic, since an argument can be made that, while analysis of a particular court may adequately describe and even explain decision making in that court, it is not necessarily representative of other courts. In other words, it is ideographic in character. The latter, of course, is a difficulty that arises whenever it seems desirable to make a statement about a population, but the only empirical evidence available is drawn from one or two case studies. This is a limitation with which researchers into the juvenile justice system simply have to live, pending the development of enough data bases to permit comparative research between courts.

The most recent and perhaps most comprehensive analysis of the detention decision is that done by Cohen (1975b) as a part of LEAA's Utilization of Criminal Justice Statistics Project. Cohen employed data from the Denver juvenile court to estimate the relationship between preadjudication detention and a number of case characteristics. It was found that the number of previous referrals was the single most important indicator of the decision, and that the relationship was in the expected direction: the greater the number of previous referrals, the more likely the detention decision was affirmative. Whether the juvenile was working, in school, or idle during the day was also relevant, but at a smaller level. Other variables, such as whether the home was intact or broken, the type of agency making the referral, the severity of offense, SES, and the age, sex, and race of the juvenile were found to be of lesser or virtually no relevance. As Cohen observed, however, there were indications in the data that different types of offense were treated differentially by the court, though these differences did not match the ranking of offense types which court personnel established as an ordinal scale of severity. For instance, alcohol, drug, and sex offenses, ranked 1, 4, and 6, respectively, on the severity scale (1 = least severe), were all subject to a higher detention rate than violent offenses, which were ranked most severe.

Cohen also cites an earlier study by Sumner (1970), based on data from several counties in California. Sumner sought to explain the variance in detention decision through the analysis of a large number of legal and nonlegal characteristics. She concluded that the following were the best indicators: number of previous referrals, type of prior offense history, history of prior detention, history of previous probation, referral as a runaway, and referral for incorrigibility.

A number of other studies have considered general juvenile

court decision making, without focusing specifically upon the prehearing detention decision. Some have suggested that legalistic variables are more important indicators than personal characteristics such as race, ethnicity, SES, or place of residence (Terry, 1967; Weiner and Willie, 1974), while others have demonstrated almost the reverse (Arnold, 1974; Meade, 1973).

The diversity of findings represented by this research may be the product of the kind of philosophical differences between decision makers that were mentioned earlier. Alternatively, it may be due to different research and analytic approaches. As Cohen (1975b:16) observed, the interaction effects between a set of independent variables can be complex and difficult to estimate without adequate multivariate analytic techniques. When, for instance, it is found that nonwhites are more often detained than whites, is it appropriate to conclude that courts are being influenced by the race of the juvenile? Not necessarily, because it may be that nonwhites commit more serious offenses than whites, and are detained for that reason. It would, therefore, be necessary to control for the type of offense committed, in order to consider this possibility. Also, it clearly is the case that other variables besides offense could account for these differential treatment practices. Consequently, a theoretically relevant set of controls must be introduced before confidence in the findings can be justified. This issue will be considered in more detail during the discussion below of the methodological approach of this paper.

METHODOLOGY

The prehearing detention decision is theoretically conceived to be a function of case characteristics, the precise form of the function presently being unknown. It is hypothesized that the function is linear. That is, the impact of characteristics on the decision is additive. It is further hypothesized that the individual relationship of any characteristic with the decision is also linear. Therefore, a suitable model for the representation of the function is as follows:

$$y = b_0 + b_1x_1 + b_2x_2 + \ldots + b_kx_k + e \qquad [1]$$

In this model, y represents the decision being investigated, while the x_i represent the case characteristics that affect the decision. The coefficients b_1-b_k represent the weight attributed to x_1-x_k, respectively. The intercept of the model (i.e., the value of y when all x_i are zero) is represented by b_0, and the effect of unspecified or excluded variables is represented by e.

The selection of variables to be included in the estimation of this model has been made on the basis of prior research findings, and as a result of discussions with court personnel. The operationalized variables are listed in Figure 1. Most of them are self-explanatory. However, a few clarifying comments are in order about the two home environment variables and about the school problems variable.

The status of the home is considered to be intact if the juvenile is living with both natural parents, and broken if at least one natural parent is absent. This does not necessarily mean that the child lives with a single parent. The stability of the home is estimated by case workers on the basis of variables other than home status. These include the following: whether there are criminal or delinquent siblings present; whether the mother or father is alcoholic or unstable mentally; whether the mother is home during times when the juvenile is not at school; whether the home is clean and has adequate space for the juvenile. Undoubtedly, there are also nonquantifiable subjective factors which influence this judgment.

Variable	Categories		
Prehearing detention	(1) None	(2) Juvenile home or jail	
Age	(1) Under 14	(2) 14-15	(3) 16-17
Sex	(1) Male	(2) Female	
Race	(1) White	(2) Nonwhite	
Status of home	(1) Intact	(2) Broken	
Stability of home	(1) Stable	(2) Unstable	
Offense	(1) Status	(2) Misdemeanor	(3) Felony
Number of previous referrals	(1) None	(2) One	(3) Two or more
School problems	(1) Few	(2) Many	

Figure 1. VARIABLES INCLUDED IN THE STUDY

School problems is an index variable, calculated from information about discipline difficulties, truancy, and absenteeism. Individuals with problems in two of these three areas are included in category (1) of school problems; individuals with fewer problems than this are included in category (2).

A verbal expression of the model expressed formally in equation [1] can now be made. In the following statement, prehearing detention corresponds to the y variable in [1], while the set of independent variables correspond to the x_1:

Prehearing Detention = f (age, sex, race, status of home, stability of home, offense, number of previous referrals, school problems)

It is common to estimate this kind of model through the use of multiple regression. This is, in fact, the procedure used by Cohen and Sumner in the works cited above. However, this technique assumes that the dependent variable is measured on an interval scale, and that error terms are normally distributed, with constant variance and a mean of zero (Draper and Smith, 1966). These assumptions are violated in analyses of variables such as those used in this study, primarily because of the restriction of the range of the dependent variable to two ordinal categories. Arguments have been made that this type of violation is more than offset by the added manipulative power of the multiple regression model (Abelson and Tukey, 1970, among others), and it is the case that much social science research utilizes interval level techniques with ordinal variables (Robinson, Rusk, and Head, 1972). Nevertheless, distortions will inevitably exist when this approach is taken, and the predictive capacity of the model must be compromised. For instance, in the analysis of the Denver court by Cohen, the regression model yields an R^2 of .096. One interpretation of this statistic is that 9.6% of the variance of the detention decision is "explained" by the model, while 90.4% remains "unexplained." Obviously, then, the predictive capacity of the model is rather low. However, from a theoretical point of view, Cohen's model seems much sounder than this interpretation suggests. The discrepancy between the theoretical statement and the empirical test may be due, in part, to the violation of the basic assumptions of the technique.

One alternative to the regression approach, which, to some extent, mitigates the kind of problems just reviewed,[2] consists of the use of an estimating technique known as Probit. This technique, originally developed by biometricians (see, especially, Finney, 1947), has been incorporated recently into social science inquiry (McKelvey and Zavoina, 1971, 1975; Aldrich and Cnudde, 1975) and is suitable as an estimator of the model expressed in equation [1]. Probit assumes that there exists an underlying linear model, which is represented by the ordinally measured dependent variable, and that this underlying model satisfies regression assumptions. Estimates are produced by the method of maximum likelihood. That is, those estimates which are most likely to have produced the observed data are selected by the estimating procedure (Goldberger, 1964).

Although Probit does not correspond precisely to regression in the development of coefficients and statistics, there are several properties which are analagous. First, it is possible to measure the overall fit of the model through the calculation of an estimated R^2. This can be interpreted, broadly, in much the same way as the comparable regression goodness of fit measure. Second, the Maximum Likelihood Estimates (MLEs), can be standardized in a manner analagous to the calculation of beta weights in regression, through the estimation of the variance of the underlying linear variable (McKelvey and Zavoina, 1975:112). It is therefore possible to draw conclusions about the relative importance of the set of independent variables included in the model.

A final desirable property of the Probit program, as developed by McKelvey and Zavoina, is that it calculates the proportion of cases predicted correctly by the model. This permits a clear and valuable interpretation of the model. What this means in the current study is that it will be possible to state the percentage of prehearing detention decisions for which the model would have made a correct prediction.

In addition to the use of the Probit estimating technique,

relationships between variables will be explicated by means of contingency tables. This will allow the display of bivariate associations, and a first order control, using the offense variable, will be introduced. Inasmuch as this approach is a lower order of analysis than a multivariate strategy, it will be completed before Probit estimates are presented. Finally, a path model of the prehearing detention decision will be presented, illustrating the interrelationships between it and the independent variables listed in Figure 1.

BASIC ASSOCIATIONS:
DETENTION AND CASE CHARACTERISTICS

Analysis of the prehearing detention decision is not appropriate for all cases that are referred to the court. Many juveniles are either dismissed by referees at the time of referral or are directed toward the Youth Services Bureau. These individuals obviously were not detained. To include them in a discussion of the detention decision, however, would seriously distort the findings, since the criteria involved in the dismissal are, in principle, different from those that affect detention. Therefore, in this study only those cases for which detention was a real possibility will be included in the analysis. There were 500 such cases. Of these, 205 were detained, while 295 were not. In all tabular presentations which follow, the total N for the category is presented, along with the percentage of that N which were detained. A suitable statistic (Goodman-Kruskall's Gamma or Yule's Q, depending on whether the variables are ordinal or nominal, respectively) is calculated as a summary of the strength of the association between the dependent variable, prehearing detention decision, and independent variable being presented in the particular table.

Detention and Offense Classification

Table 1 depicts the association between the detention decision and the classification of the offense as felony, misdemeanor, or status. The table shows that there were 167 felonies, 121 misdemeanors, and 212 status offenses among the

Table 1: PERCENTAGE OF CASES DETAINED, BY OFFENSE CLASSIFICATION

	Felony	Misdemeanor	Status	Total
(N)	(167)	(121)	(212)	(500)
%	44.9	24.0	47.6	41.0

$$G = -.071$$

500 cases subject to an affirmative or negative decision about detention. Detained were 44.9% of the felonies, 24% of the misdemeanors, and 47.6% of the status offenders. $G = -.071$, which is very weak and negative.

In the construction of this table, an assumption has been made that felonies are the most serious kinds of offenses, while status offenses are the least serious. A further assumption about court decision making was that the more serious the offense, the more severe the decision of the court. Finally, it was assumed that detention is more severe than nondetention. Logically, then, it might be anticipated that the court would detain felony offenders at a higher rate than misdemeanor offenders, and misdemeanor offenders at a higher rate than status offenders. This is not the case. The fact that the statistic is negative means that, overall, the less serious the offense, the more likely the offender is to be detained; the fact that the statistic is small means that the offense is a poor indicator of court decision making.

If only the adult offense distribution is considered, however, it is clear that the direction of the relationship is positive and is quite strong $(G = +.44)$. If status offenses are compared to misdemeanor offenses, the relationship is negative and also strong $(G = -.47)$. This same interpretation can, of course, be derived from the table by simply noting the differences in the percentage detained for the three offense classifications. Thus, in fact, offense is a good indicator of court decision making with reference to detention; it is simply not linear.

This situation has serious implications for the remainder of the analysis and also suggests one explanation for the not uncommon conclusion in other research (see above) that detention decision and offense are only weakly related. Since statistics, such as gamma, and techniques, such as regression analysis, assume linearity in associations between variables, their utility is clearly constrained if status and adult offenses are grouped together in the analysis. They are in fact likely to be very misleading. Furthermore, the fact that they are misleading will be concealed unless the precise distribution of cases can be examined as in Table 1. In regression analysis, for instance, where a single coefficient summarizes the total association, there is no way to determine from the coefficient whether or not the relationship is linear. If the coefficient is low, for instance, the relationship could be linear and weak, nonlinear and weak, or nonlinear and strong.

To compensate for this problem, the following strategy will be adopted in the present study: bivariate relationships between detention decision and case characteristics will be controlled for offense classification in order to avoid distortion; Probit analysis will focus on adult offenders as one subset, status offenders as another, and a separate model will be estimated for each subset.

To a large extent, this approach is consistent with the philosophical orientation of the juvenile justice system. Felonies and, perhaps to a lesser extent, misdemeanors are offenses against the community, status offenses are not. Thus, detention in the former cases can be justified as a move to protect the public; detention in the latter can be justified as a move to protect the individual offender. Consequently, it is to be anticipated that the determinants of decision making in the one situation will be different from those in the other. Therefore, estimating two models makes sense.

Age, Sex, and Race

Table 2 portrays the association between age, sex, race, and the detention decision for each of the three offense classifications. The point just made about the difference between adult and status offenders is strongly underlined by these data. There is a moderate, positive linear relationship between age and prehearing detention for both felony and misdemeanor (G = .226 and .346, respectively), but very little relationship for status offenders (G = .071). In other words, the older the adult

**Table 2: PERCENTAGE DETAINED BY AGE, SEX, AND RACE
CONTROLLING FOR OFFENSE CLASSIFICATION**

Offense	Felony			Misdemeanor			Status		
Age	4-13	14-15	16-17	4-13	14-15	16-17	4-13	14-15	16-17
(N)	(24)	(70)	(73)	(36)	(48)	(35)	(45)	(101)	(65)
%	29.2	44.3	50.7	13.9	25.0	34.3	40.0	51.5	47.4
		G = .226			G = .346			G = .071	
Sex	Male		Female	Male		Female	Male		Female
(N)	(146)		(21)	(79)		(42)	(116)		(96)
%	45.9		38.1	27.8		16.7	44.0		52.1
		Q = −.159			Q = −.317			Q = +.162	
Race	White		Nonwhite	White		Nonwhite	White		Nonwhite
(N)	(106)		(58)	(87)		(31)	(180)		(22)
%	43.4		48.3	24.1		25.8	47.8		63.6
		Q = .098			Q = .045			Q = .313	

offender the more likely it is that the court will decide in favor of detention. That the association is stronger for misdemeanor offenders supports the interpretation that the less serious the offense the greater the relevance of the offender's age. Examination of the status distribution shows that older offenders in this classification are also more likely to be detained, up to the age of 15 years. For 16-17 year olds, however, the detention rate drops somewhat. This seems to be a recognition by the court that, on attainment of the 18th birthday, the offense for which the individual is referred would no longer be an offense and, therefore, the value of detention seems moot.

The sex of the offender is also associated with the detention decision, and again the direction of the association differs according to offense classification. Male adult offenders are more likely to be detained than female adult offenders; but the reverse is true for status offenders. The adult level association is stronger for misdemeanors than it is for felonies. This reinforces the suggestion of leniency toward females on the part of the court, which it is more able to apply if the offense is less serious. The greater detention rate for female status offenders is perhaps consistent with a general cultural notion that boys will be boys while girls must be protected.

The association between race and detention is very weak for adult offenders. Nonwhites are slightly more likely to be detained than whites, especially for felony offenses (Q = .098). For status offenses, however, the nonwhite detention rate is considerably higher than the white (Q = .313). This is somewhat anomalous, but may be due to the perception on the part of the court that the nonwhite home situation has a greater tendency to be unstable at or around the time of the referral (Dungworth, 1976).

Number of Previous Referrals

Previous research has shown that a record of prior offenses is a strong indicator for juvenile court decisions (see above). This study supports that conclusion, as is illustrated in Table 3. The association is marked for felony offenders (G = .698) and remains quite strong for misdemeanor (G = .590) and status (G = .293) offenders. It should be observed that the number of offenders with two or more previous referrals is small in each offense type, relative to the other categories, and that this may be artificial, thus leading to a strong association, which could easily be weakened by the addition of a few cases in which the

Table 3: PERCENTAGE OF CASES DETAINED, BY NUMBER OF PREVIOUS REFERRALS, CONTROLLING FOR OFFENSE CLASSIFICATION

Felony Offenders	**Number of Previous Referrals**		
	None	One	Two+
(N)	(98)	(48)	(18)
%	28.6	66.7	83.3
		G = .698	
Misdemeanor Offenders	**Number of Previous Referrals**		
	None	One	Two+
(N)	(87)	(25)	(8)
%	17.2	28.0	87.5
		G = .590	
Status Offenders	**Number of Previous Referrals**		
	None	One	Two+
(N)	(133)	(60)	(16)
%	42.9	55.0	68.8
		G = .293	

decision went the other way. This development would, of course, be consistent with the notion of a relationship which had an upper bound. Putting it another way, it seems likely that the influence on the court of the number of previous referrals will diminish as that number increases. For instance, it probably makes little difference if an offender has five or six prior referrals; but it may make a lot of difference if the offender has none, rather than one.

Status and Stability of Home

In this study, the home is defined as intact if both natural parents are present. Otherwise, it is defined as broken. It is defined as stable or unstable by case workers on the basis of a variety of characteristics—parental stability, sibling delinquency or criminality, steady employment of the father, and others. Table 4 presents data on the distribution of cases with respect to these two variables.

Both the stability and the status of the home are associated with the detention decision in the theoretically expected direction. The greater the home stability the lesser the likelihood of detention; similarly, offenders from intact homes are detained at lower rates than those from broken homes. These associations hold for both variables, regardless of the offense classification, though it is the case that the associations are stronger for more serious offenses on a monotonic scale. The close resemblance between the relationships of the two

Table 4: PERCENTAGE OF CASES DETAINED, BY STABILITY OF HOME AND STATUS OF HOME, CONTROLLING FOR OFFENSE CLASSIFICATION

	Felony		Misdemeanor		Status	
Stability of home	Stable	Unstable	Stable	Unstable	Stable	Unstable
(N)	(65)	(44)	(46)	(41)	(90)	(68)
%	28.1	59.1	19.6	29.3	46.7	58.8
	$Q = .573$		$Q = .260$		$Q = .240$	
Status of home	Intact	Broken	Intact	Broken	Intact	Broken
(N)	(61)	(104)	(55)	(63)	(82)	(163)
%	32.8	51.9	16.4	30.2	45.1	51.2
	$Q = .378$		$Q = .376$		$Q = .122$	

home variables with the detention decision suggests that they are to some extent coterminous and raises the possibility that at least one of the associations is spurious. The multivariate analysis to be reported subsequently in this paper will test for this possibility.

In one sense, the character of both relationships is inconsistent with the trend revealed in the examination of other variables. A picture of decision making has been developing in which nonoffense variables have been most influential for less serious offenses. This trend was pronounced, for instance, for age and sex, and also existed, to a lesser degree, for race. In the case of home variables, however, the opposite situation prevails. Stability and status of the home are both more relevant for the more serious offenses. This can be seen in the summary statistic that is calculated for each classification, but it is also very obvious from looking at the percentage distribution of cases detained. The detention rate for felony offenders from unstable homes, for instance, is 59.1%; for those from stable homes it is 28.1%. This is a substantially different picture than is gained from the status offense distribution, where 58.8% from unstable homes are detained, compared to 46.7% from stable ones. The same tendency exists throughout Table 4. A logical and theoretical explanation for this finding is somewhat difficult to find. It has been suggested by Ferdinand[3] that detention may enhance the likelihood of appearance in court in situations where the home is unstable, and that this might account for the variance in the decision. It was not possible to develop the data on appearance rates which would be necessary to empirically support this explanation, but if appearance were a problem, it would certainly be plausible.

School Problems

This variable is compiled as an index from data on discipline difficulties, truancy, and absenteeism. It is expected that the greater the school problems the more likely offenders are to be detained, regardless of the offense. This position is supported by the data, though the strength of the support is much greater for adult than for status offenses. G = .474 for felonies, .647 for

Table 5: PERCENTAGE OF CASES DETAINED, BY SCHOOL PROBLEMS, CONTROLLING FOR OFFENSE CLASSIFICATION

Felony Offenders	School Problems	
	Few	Many
(N)	(50)	(51)
%	32.0	56.9
	G = .474	
Misdemeanor Offenders	School Problems	
	Few	Many
(N)	(40)	(30)
%	12.5	40.0
	G = .647	
Status Offenders	School Problems	
	Few	Many
(N)	(58)	(93)
%	44.8	58.0
	G = .256	

misdemeanors, and .256 for status offenses. The fact that the relationship in the misdemeanor category is stronger than that in the felony category is consistent with the trend in all but the home variable situations. That is, the less serious the offense the more likely it is that outside variables will influence the court. The status coefficient, lower than both of the other offense categories, does not support this picture, but it also does not contradict the argument being developed that the court views status offenses in a qualitatively different fashion than adult offenses.

SUMMARY OF FINDINGS
CONCERNING BASIC ASSOCIATIONS

All variables considered are associated with the prehearing detention decision, though, naturally, the precise nature and strength of the associations differ by variable. It has been demonstrated that decisions concerning adult offenses tend to be consistent with linear formulations of the variables, usually in the theoretically and logically expected fashion, but that decisions about status offenders often seem to weight the predictor variables in a radically different manner. One consequence of this tendency is that the offense classification is difficult to use in any prediction or explanation which depends upon assumptions of linearity between the offense type and the detention decision, unless adult and status offenders are separated into two classes for the purpose of analysis. This argument, presented during the discussion of offense classification, has been supported by the analysis of other independent variables.

With the exception of home factors, the court appears to give added weight to case characteristics, such as age, sex, and school problems, when the offense is less serious. This is consistent with the viewpoint that the juvenile justice system should avoid rigidity in its dealings with referrals and, where possible, should exercise informed discretion concerning the disposition of cases.

MULTIVARIATE MODELS

The necessity for a multivariate approach to the prediction and explanation of criminal justice phenomena has been stressed previously (Cohen, 1975a and 1975b, among others). However, the argument bears repeating. The world is not bivariate—it is multivariate—and relationships between variables tend to be complex. Consequently, efforts to understand what is taking place in agencies or on the streets are severely handicapped by the use of a strategy which looks only at the association between a dependent variable, such as prehearing detention decision, and a single independent variable. This is so even if the process is repeated for a relatively large number of independent variables. To say this does not mean that the basic relationships should be ignored. Frequently, valuable information can be obtained by careful examination of, for instance, bivariate contingency tables. A case in point was developed in the present paper with respect to the nonlinear character of the detention decision/offense association. However, the likelihood that bivariate relationships are, to some extent, spurious is so strong that it can be disregarded only with great risk. Putting the same argument another way, a bivariate formulation is a model which is highly underspecified.

It is, of course, also possible to go too far in the other direction. The inclusion of a long list of independent or predictor variables, in an equation which purports to be a multivariate explanation of the dependent variable, is not likely to yield insight into a problem unless the "list" is theoretically and logically sound, well operationalized, and interpreted through a technique which matches the variables. In other words, the construction of a model should be parsimonious, where possible, and more should not be claimed for any technique than it can deliver.

In summary, then, the argument being made here is that a sound research strategy for the kind of problem being examined in this paper is as follows: first, examine bivariate relationships, both to obtain information generally about the distribution of cases and to spot "problem" areas; second, formulate a multivariate model of the interaction between variables, which is theoretically based and which reflects the knowledge developed through bivariate analysis; third, select an analytic technique which is suited both to the formulation and to the nature of the variables included in it. The second and third steps are, of course, the focus of this section of the paper.

ANALYSIS OF THE
PREHEARING DETENTION DECISION USING PROBIT

As was discussed in the section on offense classification, cases subject to the prehearing detention decision were divided into two classes for the purposes of the multivariate analysis. Felony and misdemeanor offenders were placed in one class; status offenders were placed in another. The justification for this division lies in the nonlinear relationship of offense type with prehearing detention, when all three categories are included. This condition suggests that the court views status offenders in a different manner than adult offenders, and this idea was supported by the discussion of other variables besides offense.

There will consequently be two models—one focusing on adult offenders and one on status offenders. Each model will be estimated through the use of the Probit technique, and MLEs and estimated beta weights will be calculated for each variable. Naturally, it is anticipated that the coefficients for any given variable will differ from model to model.

The two models will differ in one important respect: offense will be included as a variable in the adult offender model, whereas it will not be a variable in the status offender model for obvious reasons.

The results of the Probit estimation for the two models are presented in Table 6. In addition to the coefficients for individual variables, summary statistics are presented on significance of the equations ($-2LLR = -2 \times$ Log of the Likelihood Ratio, which is equivalent to X^2 with the appropriate degrees of freedom); the estimated R^2, which is analogous in interpretation to the R^2 in a regression analysis; and the percentage of decisions predicted correctly from the models.

It can be seen that the adult offender model is a more successful interpretation of the detention decision than the status offender model. In the former, $R^2 = .292$, while in the latter it is .160. Similarly, the adult offender model predicts 72.1% of the detention decisions correctly, while the status model predicts 65.9% correctly. It should be remembered in the interpretation of this prediction success rate that the detention

Table 6: PROBIT ANALYSIS OF PREHEARING DETENTION

Independent Variable	Felony and Misdemeanor Offenders		Status Offenders	
	MLE	Est. Beta	MLE	Est. Beta
Age	.251	.116	.008	.004
Sex	.141	.019	.151	.035
Race	.181	.029	.470	.051
Offense	.590	.119	Not Applicable	
Status of home	.043	.009	.286	.065
Stability of home	.061	.012	.343	.080
Number of previous referrals	.447	.192	.226	.096
School problems	.081	.104	.334	.076
−2LLR	235.7* (X^2 with 8df)		94.5* (X^2 with 7df)	
Estimated R^2	.292		.160	
% predicted correctly	72.1		65.9	

*Significant at .05 level or better

decision is a dichotomous one, and that it is, therefore, possible to be correct 50% of the time through random prediction. It is also possible to be correct 59% of the time by predicting the most frequent category (nondetention).

The relative importance of the predictor variables can be derived from the estimated beta weights. For felony and misdemeanor offenders, the number of previous referrals has the greatest impact (.192), followed by offense classification (.119), age (.116), and school problems (.104). Sex and race are much less relevant (.019 and .029, respectively), and home factors are similarly unimportant. A general interpretation of the detention decision for this case of offenders, then, would be that the current and past offense record carries greater weight than other case characteristics. In particular, home factors appear to be of minimum relevance, which is surprising considering that, in the bivariate analysis, both status and stability of the home showed moderate associations with the detention decision. What this means, of course, is that the original association was spurious, due to interaction between home factors and other variables in the equation.

The conclusions to be drawn from the status offender model are somewhat different. Overall, the coefficients tend to be lower than in the adult offender model, which is to be expected since the latter is a better estimation than the former. In addition, however, the relative importance of the variables differs. The number of previous referrals (.096) is still the most important indicator, but home stability (.080) and whether or not the home is intact or broken (.065) are not far behind. School problems (.076) remain relatively important, and race (.051) is also relevant. Age and sex are least important.

In summary, then, the primary difference between the two models is that home factors are minor in the adult offender model, while they are important in the status offender model. Age is a strong factor in the adult model, but a weak one in the status model. The main similarity lies in the dominance of the number of previous referrals.

PATH MODELS OF THE DETENTION DECISION

A path model, as used in this paper, is simply a convenient visual representation of findings such as those presented in Table 6. The model depicts the main relationships between the dependent variable and the set of predictor variables incorporated in the estimation process. Path coefficients consist of the estimated beta weights calculated in the Probit analysis.

Because of the critical role of the offense classification, whether felony or misdemeanor (developed in the bivariate section of this paper and reaffirmed by the adult model), offense will be treated as a dependent variable for one section of the adult offender path model. Putting it another way, offense will be considered to be an intervening variable, with the potential of being directly affected by other case characteristics. The specific formulation is as follows:

Offense (adult only) = f (age, sex, race, status of home, stability of
home, number of previous referrals, school
problems)

The results for this model of offense commission, estimated in a previous paper which used the same data (Dungworth, 1976), are presented in Table 7. It can be seen that the critical

Table 7: PROBIT ANALYSIS OF OFFENSE[a]
FELONIES AND MISDEMEANORS ONLY

Independent Variable	MLE	Est. Beta
Age	.313	.137
Sex	.990	.129
Race	.030	.008
Status of home	.088	.017
Stability of home	.311	.058
Number of previous referrals	.754	.289
School problems	.173	.210
$-2LLR$ (X^2 with 8df)	310.78[b]	
Estimated R^2	.369	
% predicted correctly	71.2	

a. Reproduced from Dungworth, 1976.
b. Significant at .05 level or better.

variables, in order of importance, are: the number of previous referrals, school problems, age, sex, stability of the home, status of the home, and race. The model predicts 71.2% of the cases correctly, compared to the 50% that could be predicted correctly on a random basis.

The information from Tables 6 and 7 can now be combined in a path model of the detention decision for those juveniles committing felonies or misdemeanors. The model is presented in Figure 2. Variables are included in the path representation if the estimated beta weight is greater than .05. The exclusion of variables, such as race, does not mean that they have *no* effect; it simply means that the effect is very small, and that the "success" of the model is not dependent upon them to a very great degree.

The model shows that age, school problems, and the number of previous referrals are relevant both to the kind of offense committed and to the prehearing detention decision. The sex of the offender and the stability of the home have some impact on the offense, but very little upon the court's decision. The race

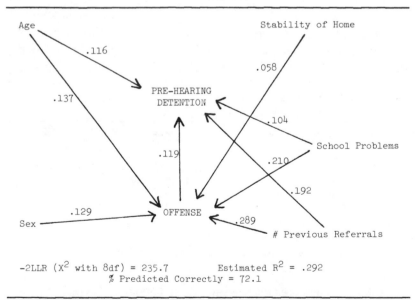

-2LLR (X^2 with 8df) = 235.7   Estimated R^2 = .292
                    % Predicted Correctly = 72.1

Figure 2. A PATH MODEL OF THE PREHEARING DETENTION DECISION FOR FELONY AND MISDEMEANOR OFFENDERS

of the offender and whether or not the home is intact or broken have little relevance either to the offense or to the detention decision.

A second path model, for status offenders only, is presented in Figure 3. The significance of home factors is clearly visible, in contrast to the situation in Figure 2. Race is also of some significance, while age and sex do not appear to be important. School problems, and especially the number of previous referrals are relevant here as they were in the adult offense model.

CONCLUSION

In this paper, the relationship between a set of case characteristics and the prehearing detention decision in the Calhoun County Juvenile Court has been investigated. It has been shown that zero order associations of varying strength exist between the detention decision and age, sex, race, offense classification, status of the home, stability of the home, number of previous referrals to the court, and the existence of problems

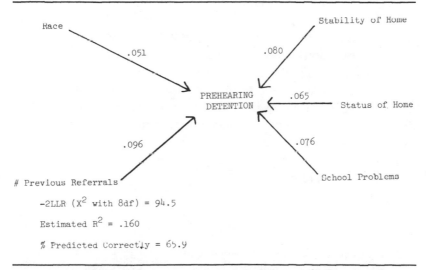

-2LLR (X^2 with 8df) = 94.5

Estimated R^2 = .160

% Predicted Correctly = 65.9

Figure 3. A PATH MODEL OF THE PREHEARING DETENTION DECISION FOR STATUS OFFENDERS

in school. Of these, the offense type and the number of previous referrals were the most important.

Multivariate analysis, using the Probit estimator, supports the conclusion that referral history and school problems are of prime importance in predicting the decision, regardless of the type of offense committed. The decision is also strongly related to offense classification, though it is not meaningful to include all three categories of offense in the analysis, since the association between offense and decision is nonlinear. This problem is handled by estimating two separate models, one for juveniles committing adult offenses, and one for those committing status offenses. The two models differ in that home factors are important for the status model, but are minor in the adult model. The two also diverge with respect to age, which is important for the adult offense decision but not for the status decision, and race, where the situation is reversed. The sex of the offender does not appear to be relevant in either model.

The general picture of court decision making that is provided by this analysis is that of a relatively high degree of "rationality" (71.2% predictable on the basis of objectively measured characteristics) in decisions about felony and misdemeanor offenders, with nonoffense characteristics being more important for decisions about the latter than about the former.

Decisions about status offenders are "rational" to a lesser degree (65.9% predictable). This may reflect a basic dilemma facing the total juvenile justice system concerning status offenders. Discretionary power is clearly greater with respect to this kind of case, since legal guidelines are much more hazy, and since there is often a need to act on very short notice, sometimes with a small amount of information about the individual being referred.

NOTES

1. For an overview of literature relevant to these issues, see Cohen, 1975b.

2. It should not be inferred from this statement that Probit is immune from other kinds of problems that plague multivariate research, including but not necessarily limited to such difficulties as multicolinearity and underspecification.

3. Private communication to the author, March 4, 1977.

REFERENCES

ABELSON, R.P., and TUKEY, J.W. (1970). "Efficient conversion of nonmetric information into metric information." In E.R. Tufte (ed.), The quantitative analysis of social problems. Reading, Mass.: Addison-Wesley.

ALDRICH, J., and CNUDDE, C.F. (1975). "Probing the bounds of conventional wisdom: A comparison of regression, Probit and discriminant analysis." American Journal of Political Science, 19(3):571-608.

ARNOLD, W.R. (1974). "Race and ethnicity relative to other factors in juvenile court dispositions." American Journal of Sociology, 77(2):211-223.

COHEN, L.E. (1975a). Juvenile dispositions. Washington, D.C.: U.S. Department of Justice.

——— (1975b). Who gets detained. Washington, D.C.: U.S. Department of Justice.

DRAPER, N.R., and SMITH, H. (1966). Applied regression analysis. New York: John Wiley.

DUNGWORTH, T. (1976). "Home, school and personal factors as predictors of juvenile offense type." Mimeo. Michigan State University.

FINNEY, D.J. (1947). Probit analysis. Cambridge: Cambridge University Press.

GOLDBERGER, A.S. (1964). Econometric theory. New York: John Wiley.

McKELVEY, R., and ZAVOINA, W. (1971). "An IBM Fortran IV program to perform N-chotomous multivariate Probit analysis." Behavioral Science, 16(March):186-187.

——— (1975). "A statistical model for the analysis of ordinal level dependent variables." Journal of Mathematical Sociology, 4:103-120.

MEADE, A. (1973). "Seriousness of delinquency, the adjudicative decision and recidivism—A longitudinal configuration analysis." Journal of Criminal Law and Criminology, 64(4):478-485.

ROBINSON, J.P., RUSK, J.G., and HEAD, K.B. (1972). Measures of political attitudes. Ann Arbor, Mich.: Institute for Social Research.

SHERIDAN, W.H. (1966). Standards for juvenile and family courts. Washington, D.C.: U.S. Department of Health, Education, and Welfare.

SUMNER, H. (1970). Locking them up. National Council on Crime and Delinquency: Western Region.

TERRY, R.M. (1967). "The screening of juvenile offenders." Journal of Criminal Law, Criminology and Police Science, 58(June):173-181.

THORNBERRY, T.P. (1973). "Race, socioeconomic status and sentencing in the juvenile justice system." Journal of Criminal Law and Criminology, 64(1):90-98.

WEINER, N.L., and WILLIE, C.V. (1974). "Decisions by juvenile officers." American Journal of Sociology, 77(2):199-210.

Thomas D. McDonald
Jeri J. Thilmony
Eldon C. Schriner
*North Dakota
State University*

3

RURAL DELINQUENTS
A Ten Year Assessment of
Their Disposition Patterns

While concern with the use of official statistics for explaining crime is long standing (see, for example, Sellin, 1931, and Turk, 1969), social scientists in the United States have been tardy in recognizing the utility of official statistics for the analysis of the patterns and policies of the criminal justice system. The well-known challenge of Kitsuse and Cicourel (1963) to token concern with the "reliability" of official "social bookkeeping data" has served, in part, to underscore the heuristic value and appropriate use of such data for investigating "how individuals . . . are organizationally processed to produce rates of deviant behavior among various segments of the population" (1963:135). It is evident that in the 14 year interim criminological research has included an increasing proportion of analysis about law enforcement (e.g., Wilson, 1968), court processing (e.g., Emerson, 1969), and corrections (e.g., Empey and Lubeck, 1971).[1] While such research has served to expand our understanding of deviance processing organizations, Barton's (1976:479) observation that "one of the most glaring areas of research inadequacy is at the level of juvenile courts" reminds us of at least one continuing need in our scientific inventory.

Our concern in this paper, then, is with those factors correlated with the court processing of juvenile delinquents (see, for example, Terry, 1967; Arnold, 1971; Scarpitti and Stephenson, 1971; Meade, 1973; Cohen, 1975). The purpose of this exploratory paper is to extend our urban based delineation of the juvenile court to the rural setting.

THE DATA SET AND SETTING

The data in this investigation were collected from one of the district juvenile courts in the State of North Dakota. It is significant to note that this district juvenile court is staffed by one person who performs multiple roles—i.e., he is the juvenile commissioner, the supervisor, the referee, and the probation officer for an eight county region of jurisdiction. Furthermore, he has occupied these positions during the entire period from which the data were collected. Prior to his present position, this person was a police chief for 17 years in the largest city of his court district. Spanning a time range of 1965 through 1974, data have been assembled on over 3,300 nontraffic juvenile court processed cases, for an annual average of approximately 2.8% of the 11,424 juveniles. While North Dakota is one of the more rural states with a 1973 estimate of 635,000 people, the jurisdiction of this court has an even lower population density with the 1973 figures estimating 41,526 residents in the eight county district. Stated differently, this longitudinal data universe is from one of the more rural regions in one of the more rural states.

Unlike previous research which has included race and socioeconomic class in an effort to determine, in part, whether differential court processing criteria may be operating, this study did not examine such factors. The reason for this omission is the absence of socioeconomic data and other social factors and the proportion of nonwhite cases for the 10 year period was negligible; for the 10 year data set, 2,685 (98.8%) were Caucasian, 8 (0.3%) were Negro, and 23 (0.9%) were Indian, with 2 (0.1%) classified as "other." Thus the universe of 2,712 court processed cases (restricted to youth who resided in the court district) prohibits the analysis of socioeconomic class and race as factors of consideration in the disposition decision.

Attention, therefore, focuses upon the disposition patterns as correlated with the variables of age, sex, reason for present referral, and whether the youth has already appeared before the court.

PREVIOUS INVESTIGATIONS

For the purpose of this paper, it is useful to review some of the previous investigations which have employed court records in exploring juvenile court disposition patterns. While additional studies exist (see Ariessohn, 1972), we have chosen these because, in our judgment, they best illustrate the problematic and uneven tenor of empirical research into juvenile court dispositions.

In 1971 Terry published an analysis of the sanctions administered to 9,023 juveniles by three different levels—the police, the probation department, and the juvenile court—of a heavily industrialized midwestern city of approximately 100,000 residents. Positively correlated with court disposition severity were the juvenile's age and the legal variables of "offense seriousness" and recidivism (Terry, 1967:178-180).

In a similar vein, Meade (1973) underscored the importance of legal factors over social factors in his random sample of 500 juvenile court disposition cases from a large southeastern metropolitan area. Meade concluded that the agency personnel appeared to "have internalized the dictums of individualized handling and official discretion to the point where systematic bias against any racial or social class group is nonexistent" (1973:484).

More recently, Cohen (1975:32) reported on the disposition patterns of 5,317 Denver juvenile court cases. Multivariate data analysis led him to conclude that legal criteria apparently have more explanatory power than status variables in accounting for variation in court dispositions. Throughout these studies, then, is the common proposition that legal factors are more impor-tant than socioeconomic factors in accounting for juvenile court disposition patterns.

Arnold (1971), however, in his analysis of 758 court cases in a middle sized southern city, found substantive ethnic variance in accorded dispositions. More exactly, Arnold contended that the majority of differential handling results from bias, i.e., "about two-thirds of the differential handling in the court studied is not explained by appropriate considerations" (1971:211).

Thornberry (1973), drawing upon the impressive birth cohort investigation of Wolfgang and his colleagues (1972), analyzed 9,601 disposition cases at the levels of police records, intake hearing files and juvenile court probation cases. Thornberry's analysis, when holding constant the two legal variables of offense seriousness and prior record, found that "blacks and low SES subjects were more likely than whites and high SES subjects to receive severe disposition" (1973:97).

Briefly summarized, studies by Terry (1967), Meade (1973), and Cohen (1975) present findings which challenge the long-standing assumption of discriminatory juvenile court decisions based mainly on social class and ethnic group membership.[2] Exceptions, however, have been provided by both Arnold (1971) and Thornberry (1973). The discrepancies in these five studies have not been satisfactorily explained.

Unlike the above reviewed studies, the research and data analysis of Scarpitti and Stephenson (1971) does not concep-tualize the issue of court disposition criteria in terms of legal variables *against* extralegal factors. In their three year research investigation of 1,210 16 and 17 year old juvenile court processed boys in a large eastern metropolitan county, Scarpitti and Stephenson (1971:150) concluded that

> the judges perform the function of sorting these cases according to "delinquency risk," based on prior delinquency history associated with socio-economic variables and with certain pertinent personality items.

Stated another way, Scarpitti and Stephenson seem to be suggesting that rather than ranking legal, social, and personal factors, the judges conceptualize the whole of the juvenile—his actions, his personality, and his environment—in arriving at a disposition. For researchers to rank legal, social, and personal variables seems to be an artificial effort, one which sets the stage for debates over issues which might be less puzzling if conceptualized and empirically researched from a holistic framework.

FINDINGS

Table 1 contains the 1965 through 1974 correlation tests (i.e., gamma values) for selected variables and the disposition patterns of the juvenile court. Attention now turns to an analysis of these findings.

The correlations between age and disposition, as can be observed in Table 1, show two central phenomena. First, eight of the 10 years present an inverse correlation between age and severity of the disposition; which is to say, the younger the age of the juvenile, the greater the likelihood of a severe disposition. This pattern, however, is subject to a temporal contingency. The 1965 through 1969 segment consistently reveals this inverse correlation. From 1970 through 1974, however, we see two years, 1970 and 1971, with a positive correlation between age and severity of disposition. The other three years, while characterized by inverse correlations, reach levels considerably weaker than the values of the 1965 through 1969 segment.

An interesting pattern is revealed by these figures. First, a previous study (Thilmony et al., 1976) of the offense referral patterns showed that the younger the offender's age the greater the likelihood of his being charged with a criminal offense, i.e., for a reason considered to be "serious." This pattern is consistent with national data reviewed by Caldwell and Black (1971:43) who have shown that "the younger the person, the more serious the offense must be to have official recognition of it." But if serious offenses result in more severe dispositions, it is reasonable to expect that younger juveniles will receive more severe court dispositions. This is exactly what we see in Table 1, at least from 1965 through 1969. Scarpitti and Stephenson (1971:147-148) lend some support to this contention since they found that "as a group, probationers were older and reformatory boys younger at the time of their first court appearance."

Table 1: CORRELATIONS BETWEEN SELECTED VARIABLES AND SEVERITY OF JUVENILE COURT DISPOSITION

Year	Age	Sex	Referral Reason	Referral Reason, Controlling for Subject's Sexual Status			Referral Reason, Controlling for Court Recidivism	
				Male	Female	Court Recidivism	No Court Recidivism	Court Recidivism
1965 (N = 238)	−.20	+.09	−.38	−.47	−.17	−.10	−.36	−.39
1966 (N = 292)	−.29	+.28	−.49	−.60	−.05	+.53	−.58	−.42
1967 (N = 381)	−.51	+.37	−.65	−.72	−.59	+.06	−.68	−.63
1968 (N = 327)	−.51	+.12	−.67	−.72	−.25	−.10	−.74	−.61
1969 (N = 237)	−.43	+.13	−.50	−.57	+.05	−.05	−.46	−.55
1970 (N = 227)	+.18	+.04	−.12	−.24	+.62	+.43	+.11	−.28
1971 (N = 270)	+.14	−.14	−.45	−.53	−.16	+.77	+.29	−.83
1972 (N = 225)	−.02	+.08	+.04	−.01	+.20	+.03	+.32	−.35
1973 (N = 259)	−.07	+.65	−.01	−.01	−.39	−.01	+.03	−.06
1974 (N = 256)	−.12	−.16	−.01	+.01	*	+.18	−.12	+.02

*A high proportion of cells with zero values generated a gamma of −1.00. This value is misleading for purposes of interpretation and was, therefore, excluded from presentation and discussion.

Turning attention to sexual status, we find a positive correlation between sex and court disposition in eight of the 10 years; that is, *girls are somewhat more likely than boys* to receive more severe dispositions. This pattern is consistent with Cohen's finding that "a larger percentage of males (50%) as opposed to females (40%) were counseled and then released" (1975:201).

We are not surprised by the direction of the relationship. Girls, it is reasonable to assume, for many years have been referred less readily than boys to a juvenile court. Pollack's (1950) well-known, and for many years widely accepted, "chivalry factor" may account for this phenomenon. On the basis of field observations and agency staff interviews, it appears even more applicable in the rural context. Assuming, then, that a "chivalry factor" has been operating, at least to some degree, it is to be expected that when girls are referred to the juvenile court it is likely to be for reasons deemed by someone in the community as "serious."

Returning to the positive relationships between age and disposition severity during the 1970s, part of the explanation may be the changing composition of male and female referrals. For example, as has been previously reported (Thilmony and McDonald, 1976:8-9), the 1970s have been characterized by an increase in criminal referrals for both boys and girls, but particularly for girls. From 1965 through 1969, 55.3% of male court referrals involved criminal cases while the percentage of girls was 28.1%. In the 1970s, however, the caseload for boys shows 66.2% referred for criminal behaviors while for girls it was 49.0% during these years. Thus, while criminal referrals for boys and girls are increasing, they are doing so at a sharper pace for girls, i.e., 3.8 times greater than for boys. This marked change during the 1970s may, then, be partially responsible for the lack of uniformity in our correlation values for the 1970s.

Regarding the relationship between reason for referral and severity of disposition, we find in Table 1 an inverse correlation in nine of the 10 years.[3] These negative gamma values suggest, as was expected, that criminal offenses are more likely to receive a more severe court disposition than status offenses.

Based on our findings and the works of other researchers, it was decided to continue with the analysis of referral reason and accorded disposition and control for the subject's sexual status.

When we control for the sex of the juvenile and correlate referral reason with court disposition, we see for males in nine of the 10 years and for females in six of the 10 years that we again find criminal offenses more likely than status offenses to be accorded a more severe court disposition. In comparing male and female dispositions, this particular set of figures does not appear to suggest that girls are more likely than boys to receive a more severe disposition. These data do not appear to agree with the findings of Gibbons and Griswold (1957:109), Terry (1967:178), Chesney-Lind (1973:54-58), and Cohen (1975:20), who report a greater likelihood for girls than boys to receive a more severe court disposition. Perhaps these different findings support Terry's suggestion that "variations that exist between agencies may be a function of the differences in orientation which characterize the agents of social control" (1967:180).

Of particular interest in Table 1 is the weakening and nonuniform relationships which exist during the 1970s. As has been seen, regarding the variables of age and sex, the figures for the 1970 through 1974 segment appear to suggest a changing context, particularly for girls who are now being referred for behaviors heretofore the central terrain of boys. Based on the data in Table 1, the increase in the proportion of females referred to court for criminal offenses does not appear to contribute substantively to the weakening and nonuniform gamma values during the 1970s.[4]

Turning to court recidivism and disposition, we see in Table 1 that the correlations lack consistency. Considering this unevenness and the results of previous studies, it was decided to explore this issue further and correlate referral reason with court disposition while controlling for court recidivism.

When we correlate the referral reason with court disposition, while holding constant whether the juvenile has previously appeared before the court, some interesting patterns emerge. First, from 1965 through 1969, regardless of previous court referral, negative correlations are consistently established between criminal offense referrals and severity of court disposition. This pattern, however, undergoes some interesting change during the first four years of the 1970s. For those youth who have never appeared before this juvenile court, a positive correlation is found between reason for referral and disposition severity. In the one year of this subgroup which does contain a negative gamma value, we see that it is of a considerably lower intensity than was the case during the five years of the 1960s. For those youth referred to the court previously, we find that, in the main, the intensity of the inverse correlation has weakened and for 1974 the gamma value is positive.

While these patterns are similar to the results of Terry (1967), Arnold (1971), Thornberry (1973), and Cohen (1975), the weakening gamma values for the 1970 subset alert us to a possible changing relationship between the juvenile court and the socio-organizational context in which it operates. More on this question later.

SUMMARY AND CONCLUSION

Summary

This exploratory paper has presented a 10 year data set on factors correlated with dispositions of a rural court. Briefly reviewed, six specific gamma sets were identified.

(1) Generally speaking, age is inversely correlated with the severity of court disposition. This reflects the tendency of younger referral cases to be charged with more serious offenses and thus to receive more severe court action.

(2) Bivariate analysis leads one to suspect that girls are more likely than boys to receive a more serious court disposition.

(3) For nine of the 10 years, referral reason is inversely correlated with court disposition. This reflects criminal offenses receiving a more severe disposition than status offenses.

(4) When we control for sex and correlate referral reason with court disposition, it is found that criminal referrals are more likely than status referrals to receive a severe disposition, i.e., in nine of the 10 years for males and six of the 10 years for females. These figures do

not lead one to suspect, then, that girls are more likely than boys to receive a more severe disposition. A deviance processing organization theme was suggested as an explanation for these patterns.

(5) The correlation between "court recidivism" and disposition was found to be quite uneven during the 10 year period.

(6) The above nonuniform profile prompted us to correlate referral reason with court disposition and control for previous court appearance of the juvenile. While the first five years reflect a tendency for criminal offenses to receive more serious court dispositions, this pattern did not always hold during the second five year component.

Conclusion

The correlation values throughout Table 1 suggest some interesting and possibly substantive differences between the 1965 through 1969 period as compared to the 1970 through 1974 segment. Possibly the differences in the gamma values between the two five year periods reflect a processual development of the complex relationship between community conditions, court personnel, and the rendered disposition.[5]

A full accounting of these statistical patterns awaits research which examines the interface of informal and formal social control mechanisms and how these influence the decision-making process and the disposition outcome of the juvenile court. It should, then, come as no surprise that explaining the uncovered patterns proceeds cautiously. An organization established on the principle of individualized justice (Matza, 1964) is not likely to yield data amenable to easy assessment by outsiders, considering the range of interacting factors involved in a juvenile's psychological, political, and sociological context. A similar thesis has been advanced in attempting to explain the decision-making behavior of Supreme Court justices (Schmidhauser and Gold, 1963:517-519) which may be applicable also to juvenile court commissioners.

It seems reasonable to consider that the second five year segment of our data set may be more consistent with principles of individualized justice than the first five year component. If so, perhaps it is due, at least in part, to the increasing integration of the juvenile court commissioner with his socio-political institutional framework. Should this be the case, it may account, in part, for the variance between the two five year periods and the variance within the second five year set.

In addition, it should be remembered that while the correlation between decision-making inputs and the disposition output remains in need of continued research, it is unlikely to be fully documented from a juvenile statistical court card (Matza, 1964). The work by Emerson (1969) may be illustrative of one research strategy necessary for supplementing the juvenile court statistical card so as to more satisfactorily account for the dependent variable.

Whether the above findings are representative of the American rural juvenile court system is unknown. Not only is additional research needed on the rural juvenile court, but the relative void in the knowledge of the rural criminal justice system in general awaits future research. Hopefully, this particular endeavor has provided some information and conception which will serve to stimulate further research.

NOTES

1. To be sure, significant works appeared about the criminal justice system before the Kitsuse and Cicourel prescription, e.g., Hakeem, 1957. The more contemporary works are cited as illustrative of some recent and intensifying trends in criminological research.

2. For a review of this long-standing proposition, see, among others, Thornberry, 1973.

3. The code categories for criminal (serious) offenses had low numerical values while the severe disposition categories were assigned high numerical values. Hence, an inverse gamma value reflects these coding artifacts and indicates a more severe disposition for a more serious offense.

4. Future research may provide more explanation of court disposition patterns by constructing some form of referral typology (see, for example, Sellin and Wolfgang, 1964, and Ferdinand and Luchterhand, 1970). Such analysis is beyond the scope of the present paper, however.

5. The impact of the 1967 Gault decision on the rural criminal justice system awaits analysis. It is possible that this noted decision may account, in part, for some of the differences between the statistical results of 1965 through 1969 and those of 1970 through 1974.

REFERENCES

ARIESSOHN, R.M. (1972). "Offense vs. offender in juvenile court." Juvenile Justice, 23(August):17-22.

ARNOLD, W.R. (1971). "Race and ethnicity relative to other factors in juvenile court dispositions." American Journal of Sociology, 77(September):211-227.

BARTON, W.H. (1976). "Discretionary decision-making in juvenile justice." Crime and Delinquency, 22(October):470-480.

CALDWELL, R.G., and BLACK, J.A. (1971). Juvenile delinquency. New York: Ronald.

CHESNEY-LIND, M. (1973). "Judicial enforcement of the female sex role: The family court and the female delinquent." Issues in Criminology, 8(fall):51-69.

COHEN, L.E. (1975). Juvenile dispositions: Social and legal factors related to the processing of Denver delinquency cases. Washington, D.C.: U.S. Government Printing Office.

EMERSON, R.N. (1969). Judging delinquents. Chicago: Aldine.

EMPEY, L.T., and LUBECK, S.G. (1971). The Silverlake Experiment. Chicago: Aldine.

FERDINAND, T.N., and LUCHTERHAND, E.G. (1970). "Inner-city youths, the police, the juvenile court, and justice." Social Problems, 17(spring):510-527.

GIBBONS, D.C., and GRISWOLD, M.J. (1957). "Sex differences among juvenile court referrals." Sociology and Social Research, 42(November-December): 106-110.

HAKEEM, M. (1957-1958). "A critique of the psychiatric approach to the prevention of juvenile delinquency." Social Problems, 5(winter):194-206.

KITSUSE, J.I., and CICOUREL, A.V. (1963). "A note on the use of official statistics. Social Problems, 11(fall):131-139.

MATZA, D. (1964). Delinquency and drift. New York: John Wiley.

MEADE, A. (1973). "Seriousness of delinquency, the adjudicative decision and recidivism—A longitudinal configuration and analysis." Journal of Criminal Law and Criminology, 64(December):478-485.

POLLACK, O. (1950). The criminality of women. New York: Barnes.

SCARPITTI, F.R., and STEPHENSON, R.M. (1971). "Juvenile court dispositions: Factors in the decision making process." Crime and Delinquency, 17(January): 142-151.

SCHMIDHAUSER, J.R., and GOLD, D. (1963). "*Stare decisis,* dissent and the background of the justices." In J.R. Schmidhauser (ed.), Constitutional law in the political process. Chicago: Rand McNally.

SELLIN, T. (1931). "The basis for a crime index." Journal of Criminal Law, Criminology, and Police Science, 22 (September):335-356.

SELLIN, T., and WOLFGANG, M.E. (1964). The measurement of delinquency. New York: John Wiley.

TERRY, R.M. (1967). "The screening of juvenile offenders." Journal of Criminal Law, Criminology, and Police Science, 58(June):173-181.

THILMONY, J.J., and McDONALD, T.D. (1976). "Rural socio-cultural change and its relationship to the female delinquent." Paper presented at the 28th Annual Meeting of the American Society of Criminology, November, Tucson, Arizona.

THILMONY, J.J., McDONALD, T.D., and SCHRINER, E.C. (1976). "The offense patterns of rural delinquents: A ten year assessment." Paper presented at the 40th

Annual Meeting of the Midwest Sociological Society, April, St. Louis, Missouri.

THORNBERRY, T.P. (1973). "Race, socioeconomic status and sentencing in the juvenile justice system." Journal of Criminal Law and Criminology, 64(March): 90-98.

TURK, A.T. (1969). Criminality and legal order. Chicago: Rand McNally.

WILSON, J.Q. (1968). "The police and the delinquent in two cities." In S. Wheeler (ed.), Controlling delinquents. New York: John Wiley.

WOLFGANG, M.E., FIGLIO, R.M., and SELLIN, T. (1972). Delinquency in a birth cohort. Chicago: University of Chicago Press.

Susan K. Datesman
Frank R. Scarpitti
University of Delaware

4

UNEQUAL PROTECTION FOR MALES AND FEMALES IN THE JUVENILE COURT

Ostensibly, juvenile and family courts were established as specialized tribunals for the protection of child offenders.[1] Under the *parens patriae* doctrine, the juvenile court was to provide for the care, protection, and treatment of the child in place of the natural parents. In 1909, a leading juvenile court judge wrote that the doctrine of *parens patriae* allows the court "to take [the child] in hand and instead of first stigmatizing and then reforming it, to protect it from the stigma [of criminality]" (Mack, 1909:109). The proceedings and dispositions of the juvenile court were, therefore, not supposed to be either criminal or punitive in nature. The purpose of the juvenile court was not to adjudicate guilt and mete out punishment but instead to help the child see the error of his or her ways and to offer "treatment" and "rehabilitation" before more serious criminal pursuits were undertaken. Due process safeguards were considered unimportant and juvenile court judges were granted wide discretion since it was assumed that the court was acting on behalf of the child and for the child's best interest. Consequently, not only children whose behavior contravened criminal statutes were eligible to "benefit" from the rehabilitative services offered by the juvenile court, but also children whose behavior gave evidence of delinquent tendencies.

Anthony Platt (1969) has demonstrated, however, that the motives of early reformers were less humanitarian than has often been supposed. In his important study, *The Child Savers,* Platt discusses the invention of delinquency as a legal category at the turn of the century. The imposition of normative restraints on children constituted the main thrust of the child-saving movement:

> Many of the child savers' reforms were aimed at imposing sanctions on conduct unbecoming youth and disqualifying youth from the benefit of adult privileges. . . . Their central interest was in the normative behavior of youth—their recreation, leisure, education, outlook on life, attitudes to authority, family relationships, and personal morality. [Platt, 1969:99]

Many acts of juveniles that had previously not been reacted to or had been handled informally now came under the auspices of the state. It is significant that the first law defining juvenile delinquency (in Illinois in 1899) specifically authorized penalties for predelinquent as well as delinquent behavior (Platt, 1969:138).

Acts which are predelinquent are termed juvenile status offenses, since only juveniles can commit them. Juvenile status offenses include such vague and broadly defined behavior as ungovernability, incorrigibility, and immorality. Typical of such broadly phrased delinquency statutes is Maine's, which says that the court may treat as an offender any juvenile "living in circumstances of manifest danger of falling into habits of vice and immorality." Similar delinquency statutes existed in 41 states in 1969.[2] Recently, several of these state statutes have been struck down as unconstitutionally vague, but others have withstood constitutional challenge.[3]

Unhappily, the reality of the juvenile court has fallen far short of the protective, rehabilitative rhetoric of the child savers. In practice, the legal processing of juveniles is highly stigmatizing and punitive. Despite the euphemistic terminology, the delinquent label "has come to involve only slightly less stigma than the term 'criminal' applied to adults" (*In re Gault,* 1967:27) and adjudication as a delinquent infringes on the rights of juveniles and curtails their freedom no less than a criminal conviction. In recognition of this reality, the United States Supreme Court extended minimum procedural safeguards to juvenile proceedings in the *Kent* (1966), *Gault* (1967), and *Winship* (1970) decisions. The right to trial by jury, however, is not available to juveniles (*McKeiver,* 1971). Also, recent studies concerned with the impact of *Gault* have shown that many juvenile courts have failed to fully comply with due process requirements (Lefstein et al., 1969; Langley, 1972), particularly in the case of status offenders (Finkelstein et al., 1973). Moreover, these decisions did not touch upon what rights a juvenile has in the preadjudication phase or the postadjudication or disposition stage.

There exists, therefore, a great potential for the unequal and discriminatory treatment of adolescents brought before the juvenile court. The Task Force Report on Juvenile Delinquency and Youth Crime noted that broadly written delinquency statutes, especially when administered with procedural informality, "establish the judge as arbiter not only of the behavior but also of the morals of every child. . . . The situation is ripe for over-reaching, for imposition of the judge's own code of youthful conduct" (President's Commission on Law Enforcement and Administration of Justice, 1967:25). The considerable discretion granted juvenile court judges to make moral judgments would appear to pose a greater danger to female juveniles than males. Given that the limits of acceptable behavior are much narrower for females than males, judges may mete out more severe dispositions to female juveniles who appear before them than males. And indeed, what little data we have indicate that this is the case.

Gibbons and Griswold (1957), for example, found that males and females in the state of Washington were dismissed from juvenile court jurisdiction in about the same proportions, but that females were more likely to be institutionalized than males. A study by Terry (1967) in Wisconsin found that while females were placed under informal supervision by the probation department more often than males, females brought before the juvenile court were more often sent to an institution. Finally,

Chesney-Lind (1973), in her study of the Honolulu juvenile court, found that female juveniles were less likely to be immediately released and more likely to be institutionalized than males.

These few available studies do not necessarily reveal a sex bias, however, since many considerations influence a judge's disposition. We might logically expect legal factors, such as type of offense and prior offense record, to influence the relationship between sex and disposition. Unfortunately, the studies of Gibbons and Griswold and Chesney-Lind did not use legal variables as controls in their analysis, and while Terry did control for legal factors, his analysis does not allow an examination of the contingent associations within subcategories of the legal variables. The present study attempts to overcome these handicaps by exploring the relationship between sex and disposition while accounting for the influence of instant offense type and previous record.[4]

FINDINGS

The data presented in this paper were obtained from the court records of 1,103 juveniles appearing before the family court of a medium-sized city in an eastern state during a 7-month period. The sample consists of 103 white females, 97 black females, 559 white males, and 344 black males. First, it may be noted that half of the females referred to the family court but only one-fifth of the males were charged with juvenile status offenses—running away, ungovernability, truancy, and curfew violation.[5] It may be noted further that 68% of the females as compared with 54% of the males were appearing before the court for the first time. Even so, females received somewhat harsher dispositions from the court than males (Table 1), although the relationship is of small magnitude (gamma = +.11).

When type of offense is introduced as a control on the original relationship between sex and disposition, some interesting findings emerge (Table 2). A negative relationship is found to exist between sex and disposition for felons (gamma =

−.47) and misdemeanants (gamma = −.14) while a positive relationship obtains for status offenders (gamma = +.45). That is, in the case of felonies and misdemeanors female juveniles receive a more lenient disposition while in the case of status offenses males receive a more lenient disposition. Among juveniles referred for felonies, twice as many females (65%) as males (32%) were dismissed or warned. This difference is maintained, although the margin is not as great, for females (64%) and males (55%) referred for misdemeanors. However, this pattern is reversed among status offenders: males were more than twice as likely (41%) as females (17%) to be dismissed or warned. It is interesting that in no case are the percentage differences between males and females sentenced to an institution greater than 4%, although the direction of these differences is consistent with the general pattern. Female juveniles brought before the court as status offenders were least likely to be dismissed or warned and most likely to be placed under supervision by a probation officer and institutionalized.

In Table 3, the dispositions handed out to first offenders, controlling for type of offense, are presented. Among felony offenders with no prior records of delinquent behavior, 71% of

Table 1: FAMILY COURT DISPOSITION BY SEX

Disposition	Male	Female
Dismissed	9.2% (78)	7.3% (13)
Warned	34.1% (289)	33.3% (59)
Fined	10.0% (85)	1.7% (3)
Unsupervised probation	6.6% (56)	8.5% (15)
Probation officer	33.5% (284)	41.8% (74)
Public institution	6.6% (56)	7.3% (13)
Total percent	100% (848)	100% (177)
Gamma	+.11	

Table 2: FAMILY COURT DISPOSITION BY OFFENSE TYPE AND SEX

Disposition	Felony		Misdemeanor		Status Offense	
	Male	Female	Male	Female	Male	Female
Dismissed	8.1%	14.7%	10.1%	13.6%	5.8%	0.0%
	(23)	(5)	(29)	(6)	(9)	(0)
Warned	23.9%	50.0%	44.8%	50.0%	35.3%	16.9%
	(68)	(17)	(128)	(22)	(55)	(14)
Fined	3.5%	0.0%	11.2%	2.3%	0.6%	0.0%
	(10)	(0)	(32)	(1)	(1)	(0)
Unsupervised probation	9.5%	17.6%	5.9%	13.6%	5.1%	2.4%
	(27)	(6)	(17)	(6)	(8)	(2)
Probation officer	46.0%	11.8%	23.8%	20.5%	44.9%	68.7%
	(131)	(4)	(68)	(9)	(70)	(57)
Public institution	9.1%	5.9%	4.2%	0.0%	8.3%	12.0%
	(26)	(2)	(12)	(0)	(13)	(10)
Total percent	100%	100%	100%	100%	100%	100%
	(285)	(34)	(286)	(44)	(156)	(83)
Gamma	−.47		−.14		+.45	

the females were dismissed or warned whereas only 34% of the males were so handled (gamma = −.52). A similar although weaker difference is shown for female (76%) and male (64%) misdemeanants with no records of previous offenses (gamma = −.21). Again, just the opposite obtains among status offenders with no records of prior delinquent behavior: the percentages dismissed or warned are 23% for females but 38% for males (gamma = +.37). The percentage differences between males and females sentenced to an institution are negligible for all three offense types.

Among status offenders who have a record of one or more previous offenses,[6] the harsher treatment of female juveniles is even more apparent (gamma = +.60). None of the female juveniles were dismissed as compared with 10% of the males; the percentages warned were 7% and 34%, respectively. In contrast, 71% of the females and 40% of the males were given supervision by a probation officer, and 21% of the females but only 13% of the males received institutionalization.

It appears, then, that males receive harsher dispositions than females for criminal offenses, but that females receive harsher dispositions than males for noncriminal status offenses, especi-

Table 3: FAMILY COURT DISPOSITION BY OFFENSE TYPE AND SEX
FOR FIRST OFFENDERS

Disposition	Felony		Misdemeanor		Status Offense	
	Male	Female	Male	Female	Male	Female
Dismissed	6.5%	16.7%	12.0%	16.2%	2.3%	0.0%
	(10)	(4)	(18)	(6)	(2)	(0)
Warned	27.5%	54.2%	52.0%	59.5%	36.0%	23.1%
	(42)	(13)	(78)	(22)	(31)	(12)
Fined	3.9%	0.0%	8.7%	0.0%	1.2%	0.0%
	(6)	(0)	(13)	(0)	(1)	(0)
Unsupervised probation	11.1%	12.5%	5.3%	13.5%	7.0%	1.9%
	(17)	(3)	(8)	(5)	(6)	(1)
Probation officer	49.0%	12.5%	21.3%	10.8%	48.8%	67.3%
	(75)	(3)	(32)	(4)	(42)	(35)
Public institution	2.0%	4.2%	0.7%	0.0%	4.7%	7.7%
	(3)	(1)	(1)	(0)	(4)	(4)
Total percent	100%	100%	100%	100%	100%	100%
	(153)	(24)	(150)	(37)	(86)	(52)
Gamma	−.52		−.21		+.37	

ally when they are repeat offenders. Research has indicated that stereotypes may influence the application of delinquent labels. Garrett and Short (1975), for example, found that social class and delinquency are strongly linked in the view of police. Police see lower-class boys as more likely to be involved in delinquent behavior than middle-class boys. Similarly, the disparate treatment which males and females are afforded by the juvenile court may reflect stereotypic notions about proper sex role behavior. Females are supposed to be delicate and frail and in need of male protection. Thus, it may be the case that relative to males, female juveniles are advantaged with respect to criminal offenses because chivalrous judges, who are mostly male, view them as weaker, less responsible, less dangerous, and more likely to be harmed by a harsh disposition.[7]

In the case of status offenses, however, stereotypic notions may work to the disadvantage of female juveniles. Running away, incorrigibility, truancy, and similar designations commonly constitute euphemisms for sexual offenses—"The underlying vein of many of these offenses is sexual misconduct by the girl delinquent" (Vedder and Somerville, 1970:147). Male juveniles are allowed a greater latitude of freedom in sexual behavior than are females. Through the socialization process, girls are taught that the female is inherently less sexual than the male, that sex cannot be enjoyed outside of a love (and preferably a marriage) context, and that it is incumbent upon them to impose sexual restraints, to be, as Margaret Mead has put it, "the conscience for two" (1949:280). Boys, on the other hand, are taught that they have strong sex drives, that sex per se is pleasurable, and that they should "go as far" with girls as possible. Therefore, censure is diverted away from the male and onto the female who is sexually active.[8] In view of this double standard of sexual morality, the more severe dispositions made by the juvenile court against female status offenders can perhaps be understood.

It is interesting to note a parallel between the disparate treatment male and female juveniles are afforded by the juvenile court for criminal and status offenses and sex-based discrimination in juvenile delinquency statutes. For example, in Oklahoma until 1972, females under 18 who committed crimes were allowed to be processed as juveniles, but juvenile proceedings were limited to males under 16. The Oklahoma Supreme Court upheld the constitutionality of the statute against an equal protection challenge on the grounds that it exemplified a legislative judgment "premised upon the demonstrated facts of life" (*Lamb* v. *State,* 1970). The United States Court of Appeals for the Tenth Circuit reversed, declaring that the statute violated the equal protection clause. The federal court did not find the unexplained "demonstrated facts" helpful in finding a rational justification for the unequal treatment accorded 16-18 year old males and 16-18 year old females (*Lamb* v. *Brown,* 1972).

By contrast, some states have determined that female juveniles require more "protection" from "immoral" but noncriminal conduct than males. Connecticut law until 1972 authorized the imprisonment of unmarried females between 16 and 21 if they were "in manifest danger of falling into habits of vice" or "leading a vicious life," but did not proscribe this type of behavior when engaged in by males of the same age group. In

1966, in *Connecticut* v. *Mattiello,* a Connecticut circuit court upheld the constitutionality of the statute against a claim of vagueness by reasoning that the safeguards of due process were inapplicable since the objective was to protect young females rather than to punish them.

Attention is directed next to Table 4, where the effects of offense type, race, and sex are simultaneously considered. These findings show the same general pattern as in Table 2. Relative to males in the same race category, females are accorded less severe treatment in the case of felonies and misdemeanors but more severe treatment in the case of status offenses. However, there are some interesting differences.

In general, the discrepancy between the dispositions given males and females brought before the court on felony and misdemeanor charges is less for blacks than whites. Among blacks referred for felonies and misdemeanors, the gamma coefficients are −.39 and −.08, respectively, while the comparable coefficients for whites are −.61 and −.20. Among blacks, 61% of the female felons were dismissed or warned as compared with 36% of the male felons, giving a difference of 25 percentage points. Among whites, 55% of the female felons and 29% of the male felons were dismissed or warned, giving a difference of 44 percentage points. The percentage differences between male and female felons sentenced to an institution are about the same for both blacks (5%) and whites (6%).

Among misdemeanants, there can be observed a 2% difference between black males and females dismissed or warned as contrasted with a 13% difference between their white counterparts. The exception to this pattern is institutionalization, where females are treated more like males among whites (difference = 1%) than among blacks (difference = 9%). The overall pattern holds when considering only misdemeanants who are first offenders where the famma coefficients are −.15 for blacks and −.25 for whites.

Additional computations on the data presented in Table 4 reveal that racial differences are weaker among males referred for felonies (gamma = +.02) and misdemeanors (gamma = +.13) than among their female counterparts (gamma = +.19 and +.27,

Table 4: FAMILY COURT DISPOSITION BY OFFENSE TYPE, RACE, AND SEX

Disposition	Felony				Misdemeanor				Status Offense			
	Black		White		Black		White		Black		White	
	Male	Female	Male	Female	Male	Female	Male	Female	Male	Female	Male	Female
Dismissed	9.9% (12)	13.0% (3)	6.7% (11)	18.2% (2)	11.1% (12)	11.1% (2)	9.6% (17)	15.4% (4)	9.2% (7)	0.0% (0)	2.5% (2)	0.0% (0)
Warned	26.4% (32)	47.8% (11)	22.0% (36)	54.5% (6)	42.6% (46)	44.4% (8)	46.1% (82)	53.8% (14)	50.0% (38)	14.6% (6)	21.3% (17)	19.0% (8)
Fined	2.5% (3)	0.0% (0)	4.3% (7)	0.0% (0)	0.0% (0)	5.6% (1)	18.0% (32)	0.0% (0)	1.3% (1)	0.0% (0)	0.0% (0)	0.0% (0)
Unsupervised probation	5.8% (7)	21.7% (5)	12.2% (20)	9.1% (1)	11.1% (12)	5.6% (1)	2.8% (5)	19.2% (5)	1.3% (1)	4.9% (2)	8.8% (7)	0.0% (0)
Probation officer	41.3% (50)	8.7% (2)	49.4% (81)	18.2% (2)	25.9% (28)	33.3% (6)	22.5% (40)	11.5% (3)	23.7% (18)	65.9% (27)	65.0% (52)	71.4% (30)
Public institution	14.0% (17)	8.7% (2)	5.5% (9)	0.0% (0)	9.3% (10)	0.0% (0)	1.1% (2)	0.0% (0)	14.5% (11)	14.6% (6)	2.5% (2)	9.5% (4)
Total percent	100% (121)	100% (23)	100% (164)	100% (11)	100% (108)	100% (18)	100% (178)	100% (26)	100% (76)	100% (41)	100% (80)	100% (42)
Gamma	-.39		-.61		-.08		-.20		+.54		+.34	

respectively). That is, in the case of felonies and misdemeanors, black females relative to white females receive more severe dispositions than black males relative to white males.

The above findings may reflect the fact that male and female roles are less differentiated among lower-class blacks than among middle-class whites.[9] Rainwater (1970: 164-166) states that lower-class black families are matrifocal in type and center around feminine authority, feminine equality, and male marginality whether the husband is absent or present in the family unit. Matrifocal means that "the continuing existence of the family is focused around the mother, that the father is regarded (to a greater or lesser degree) as marginal to the continuing family unit composed of mother and children" (Rainwater, 1970: 164). The matrifocal emphasis in family and kinship systems derives from the fact that many black females have been forced to share or assume the financial responsibilities for their families because of structural impediments which lessen the economic viability of black men (see Liebow, 1967).

Consequently, included in the socialization of black females is an attempt to prepare them for the contingency that black males might not be able to support their families entirely. Thus Rainwater points out that:

> The female role models available to girls emphasize an exaggerated self-sufficiency (from the point of view of the middle class) and the danger of allowing oneself to be dependent on men for anything that is crucial. [1966: 199]

And Ladner observes that: "In sum, women were expected to be *strong* and parents socialized their daughters with this intention because they never knew what the odds were for them having to utilize this resourcefulness in later life" (1971: 131). It appears that the traditional division of labor which assigns females the major role of housewife and excludes them from the labor market is less tenable among blacks than among whites. The passivity and dependency aspects of the female role are de-emphasized in the socialization of black females since these traits would prove dysfunctional for enabling them to

Table 5: FAMILY COURT DISPOSITION BY PRIOR DELINQUENT INVOLVEMENT (0 or 1 or more incidents), RACE, AND SEX FOR STATUS OFFENDERS

| | 0 | | | | 1+ | | | |
| | Black | | White | | Black | | White | |
Disposition	Male	Female	Male	Female	Male	Female	Male	Female
Dismissed	3.3% (1)	0.0% (0)	1.8% (1)	0.0% (0)	13.0% (6)	0.0% (0)	4.2% (1)	0.0% (0)
Warned	56.7% (17)	20.0% (4)	25.0% (14)	25.0% (8)	45.7% (21)	10.5% (2)	12.5% (3)	0.0% (0)
Fined	3.3% (1)	0.0% (0)	0.0% (0)	0.0% (0)	0.0% (0)	0.0% (0)	0.0% (0)	0.0% (0)
Unsupervised probation	0.0% (0)	5.0% (1)	10.7% (6)	0.0% (0)	2.2% (1)	0.0% (0)	4.2% (1)	0.0% (0)
Probation officer	26.7% (8)	60.0% (12)	60.7% (34)	71.9% (23)	21.7% (10)	73.7% (14)	75.0% (18)	66.7% (6)
Public institution	10.0% (3)	15.0% (3)	1.8% (1)	3.1% (1)	17.4% (8)	15.8% (3)	4.2% (1)	33.3% (3)
Total percent	100% (30)	100% (20)	100% (56)	100% (32)	100% (46)	100% (19)	100% (24)	100% (9)
Gamma	+.56		+.22		+.55		+.89	

cope with the exigencies of marriage. Thus Axelson found a greater acceptance of working wives among black males than among white males and suggests that "the dominating white culture, more than the Negro subculture, has a well-defined set of normative sanctions supporting the role of wife and mother" (1970:459).

It appears that black females as a group are more likely to violate stereotypic notions of proper female behavior than whites. Therefore, we suggest that judges may deal more severely with black female juveniles who are charged with criminal acts than with their white counterparts because they view black females as less wedded to the female role and hence as less in need of protection.[10] At the same time, it appears that black females still receive some measure of consideration relative to black males when the offense is criminal because they are female.

Turning now to status offenses, gamma coefficients of +.54 for blacks and +.34 for whites indicate that black males and females are given less comparable dispositions than white males and females. Among blacks, a 44% difference to the disadvantage of females was found between males (59%) and females (15%) who were dismissed or warned for status offenses. Among whites, the comparable percentages are 24% and 19%, giving a difference of only 5 percentage points. About 15% of black males and females were institutionalized as compared with 3% of white males and 10% of white females. Further examination of the data reveal that racial differences in court dispositions are greater among male status offenders (gamma = +.10). That is, white males are accorded more severe dispositions than black males while black females are treated more severely than white females, although the differences for females were very small.

When prior delinquent involvement is held constant, the coefficients for blacks are +.56 for first offenders and +.55 for repeat offenders as compared with +.22 and +.89 for whites (Table 5). Although the small N's caution against firm conclusions, it appears that, while status offenders with prior records are given more severe dispositions than first offenders for all sex-race groups, the disparity in treatment is particularly large for white female juveniles. Without exception, white female status offenders with prior records of delinquent behavior receive either supervision by a probation officer or institutionalization.

It is interesting to note that black males are given less harsh dispositions for juvenile status offenses than any other group. Such a finding is consistent with Reiss's observation that:

> Upper- and particularly middle-status persons in American society are regarded as the guardians of morality; women are so regarded more than men. . . . Proscribed sexual relations between parties who have a low social status, such as Negroes, criminals, or "low class," are more readily accepted than proscribed sexual acts between whites, conformers, or middle-class persons. [1960:319]

Thus, status offenders who are white and/or female may be treated more harshly because the departure from normative expectations is greater for them than for blacks and/or males. It follows that white females should receive the harshest dispositions and black males the most lenient dispositions, which is the case in our data, at least for repeat offenders.

SUMMARY AND DISCUSSION

The data of the present study indicate that the family court makes less severe dispositions against female juveniles than against males when they are involved in a criminal offense but more severe dispositions against females than males when they are involved in a noncriminal status offense, especially when they have a prior offense record. This pattern holds for both blacks and whites. However, the court tends to give more similar dispositions to black males and females than to white males and females when the offense is criminal. Among status offenders, black males receive the most lenient treatment while white females who are repeat offenders receive the most severe treatment.

It appears that the differences in the dispositions handed out to males and females by the family court may be explained in part by the differences between the roles ascribed to females and those ascribed to males. Females are supposed to be weaker, less responsible, and less dangerous than males, and they are thought to require greater protection. Because of these role differences, judges, who are usually men, may regard the criminal acts committed by female juveniles less seriously than those committed by their male counterparts, and may be more reluctant to deal harshly with them. However, sex-role definitions may work to the disadvantage of female juveniles referred to court for status offenses, usually implying sexual delinquency. Since greater moral censure attaches to female juveniles involved in sex-related offenses than to males, judges may feel that greater legal censure is warranted as well.

These findings suggest that the juvenile court has utilized its discretionary power in the service of traditional sex roles. Thus, while particular female juveniles referred to the court for criminal offenses may benefit in the short term, the long-term effect is the same—to reinforce and perpetuate outmoded sex roles. In the final analysis, the juvenile court appears to be less concerned with the protection of female offenders than the protection of the sexual status quo. Double standard treatment in the juvenile court on the basis of sex cannot be tolerated in a society committed to achieving equality of rights for males and females.

The unequal treatment of male and female juveniles by the court is part of the more general problem of injustice in juvenile proceedings. It is evident that the juvenile court has failed to fulfill the high hopes of *parens patriae* The Task Force Report states: "The great hopes originally held for the juvenile court have not been fulfilled. It has not succeeded significantly in rehabilitating delinquent youth, in reducing or even stemming the tide of juvenile criminality, or bringing justice and compassion to the child offender" (President's Commission, 1967:7).

Obviously, the juvenile court system is badly in need of reform. A major first step would be to remove status offenders from the jurisdiction of the juvenile court, as advocated by the President's Commission and the National Council on Crime and

Delinquency. The harsh dispositions meted out to status offenders, particularly when they are female, are clearly disproportionate to their "crimes," which are perhaps better viewed as "problems of growing up" (Lerman, 1971:39). Problems of growing up may be more effectively handled outside the juvenile court. Along this line, the Juvenile Justice and Delinquency Prevention Act of 1974 has funded states to develop community-based alternatives to traditional forms of detention and institutionalization.

Removing status offenders from juvenile court jurisdiction would allow the court to focus its attention and resources on juveniles who have committed serious criminal acts. The constitutional protections accorded adults facing criminal prosecution should then be extended to juvenile court proceedings. The recent Supreme Court holding in *Breed* v. *Jones* (1975) is therefore encouraging. In *Breed,* the court held that a juvenile transferred to stand trial as an adult after adjudication for the same offense in juvenile court is subject to double jeopardy. Also, criminal procedural safeguards must be applied to all stages of the juvenile court process. Perhaps then equal protection and equal punishment for both sexes will be closer to realization in the juvenile court.

NOTES

1. Discussions of the juvenile court's history, philosophy, and operation may be found in, e.g., Dunham (1958), Caldwell (1961), President's Commission on Law Enforcement and Administration of Justice (1967), Kittrie (1971:102-168), Haskel and Yablonsky (1974:389-415).

2. See *Baylor Law Review* (1969:352, 358-359, 369-371). See also *Yale Law Journal* (1973:745).

3. In 1973, the Supreme Judicial Court of Maine upheld the Maine statute in *S.S.* v. *State,* 229 A.2d 560 (1973), concluding that the statute was "sufficiently definite to withstand constitutional attack on grounds of vagueness" at 579. Similar cases are *United States* v. *Meyers,* 143 F. Supp. 1 (D. Alaska 1956); *People* v. *Deibert,* 117 Cal. App. 2d 410, 256 P. 2d 355 (2d Dist. 1953); *E.S.G.* v. *State,* 447 S.W. 2d 225 (1969), *cert. denied* 398 U.S. 956 (1970). However, several states have struck down such statutes as unconstitutionally vague, e.g., *Gonzalez* v. *Mailliard,* Civil No. 50424 (N.D. Calif., filed February 9, 1971); *Gesicki* v. *Oswald,* Civil No. 71-3276 (S.D.N.Y., filed December 22, 1971); *In re Brinkley,* J 1365-73 (D.C. Super. Ct., June 14, 1973).

4. In the analysis of our findings, gamma and partial gamma coefficients are used to assess the strength of the relationships. The legal variables are controlled by subdivision, and the relationship between sex and family court disposition is examined within these subcategories.

5. It is interesting to note that studies of self-reported delinquency show no such discrepancy between the types of delinquent behavior engaged in by males and females. Status offenses such as running away and ungovernability are frequently used as cover charges to avoid the stigma of a sexual offense (Reiss, 1960). Gold (1970) found that sex offenses, running away, and incorrigibility accounted for only 8% of the total delinquent acts reported by girls and 6% of the offenses reported by boys. Hindelang (1971) found that engaging in promiscuous sexual behavior contributed only 4% to the total delinquencies reported by girls and 8% to the offenses reported by boys. In general, self-reported studies of delinquency indicate that, while boys report a much higher proportion of delinquencies than girls, the pattern of female delinquent conduct closely parallels that of males. Why, then, are so many female juveniles referred to the juvenile court for status offenses? First, it is probable that a parental request for court intervention is far more likely to occur in the case of a daughter who is sexually active than in the case of a son (see Andrews and Cohn, 1974:1395, n.83, 88; 1397, n.95). Second, there is some evidence to suggest that police are less likely to arrest girls than boys involved in criminal offenses but more likely to arrest girls than boys involved in sexual offenses (Monahan, 1970).

6. The number of females in our sample was not large enough to allow a meaningful comparison with males in the case of felons and misdemeanants with prior offense records.

7. Unfortunately, we have no data on whether in fact judges do hold these stereotypical beliefs about females and, if so, to what extent they influence actual behavior. However, the sexist attitudes of judges are patently apparent in many statutes and court cases. See, for example, Johnston and Knapp (1971) and Frankel (1973).

8. The double standard of sexual morality has sometimes been formalized in juvenile delinquency statutes. See, for example, *Patricia A. v. City of New York* (1972).

9. Blacks were overwhelmingly concentrated in the lower half of the income distribution for the total sample while whites were concentrated in the upper half.

10. In addition, some of the harsher treatment given black females may reflect the fact that the larcenies and assaults they commit are of a more serious nature than those of white females; unfortunately, the data do not allow an assessment of this possibility.

CASES

Breed v. Jones, 421 U.S. 519 (1975).

[In re] Brinkley, J 1365-73 (D.C. Super. Ct., June 14, 1973).

Connecticut v. Mattiello, 4 Conn. Cir. Ct. 55 (1966), *cert. denied* 395 U.S. 202 (1969).

E.S.G. v. State, 447 S.W. 2d 255 (1969), *cert. denied* 398 U.S. 956 (1970).

[In re] Gault, 387 U.S. 1 (1967).

Gesicki v. Oswald, Civil No. 71-3276 (S.D.N.Y., filed December 22, 1971).

Gonzalez v. Mailliard, Civil No. 50424 (N.D. Calif., filed February 9, 1971).
Kent v. United States, 363 U.S. 541 (1966).
Lamb v. Brown, 456 F.2d 18 (1972).
Lamb v. State, 475 P.2d 829 (1970).
McKeiver v. Pennsylvania, 402 U.S. 528 (1971).
Patricia A. v. City of New York, 335 N.Y.S.2d 33 (1972).
People v. Deibert, 117 Cal. App. 2d 410, 256 P.2d 355 (2d Dist. 1953).
S.S. v. State, 299 A.2d 560 (1973).
United States v. Meyers, 143 F. Supp. 1 (D. Alaska 1956).
[In re] Winship, 397 U.S. 358 (1970).

REFERENCES

ANDREWS, R.H., Jr., and COHN, A.H. (1974). "Ungovernability: The unjustifiable jurisdiction." Yale Law Journal, 83(June):1383-1409.
AXELSON, L.J. (1970). "The working wife: Differences in perception among Negro and white males." Journal of Marriage and the Family, 32(August):457-464.
Baylor Law Review (1969). Comment, " 'Delinquent child': A legal term without meaning." 21:352-371.
CALDWELL, R.G. (1961). "The juvenile court: Its development and some major problems." Journal of Criminal Law, Criminology, and Police Science, 51(January/February):493-511.
CHESNEY-LIND, M. (1973). "Judicial enforcement of the female sex role: The family court and the female delinquent." Issues in Criminology, 8(fall):51-59.
DUNHAM, H.W. (1958). "The juvenile court: Contradictory orientations in processing offenders." Law and Contemporary Problems, 23(summer):508-527.
FINKELSTEIN, M.M., WEISS, E., COHEN, S., FISHER, S.Z. (1973). Prosecution in the juvenile courts: Guidelines for the future. Washington, D.C.: U.S. Government Printing Office.
FRANKEL, L.J. (1973). "Sex discrimination in the criminal law: The effect of the Equal Rights Amendment." American Criminal Law Review, 11(winter):469-510.
GARETT, M., and SHORT, J., Jr. (1975). "Social class and delinquency: Predictions and outcomes of police-juvenile encounters." Social Problems, 22(February):368-383.
GIBBONS, D.C., and GRISWOLD, M.J. (1957). "Sex differences among juvenile court referrals." Sociology and Social Research, 42(November/December):106-110.
GOLD, M. (1970). Delinquent behavior in an American city. Belmont, Calif.: Brooks/Cole.
HASKELL, M.R., and YABLONSKY, L. (1974). Crime and delinquency. Chicago: Rand McNally.
HINDELANG, M.J. (1971). "Age, sex, and the versatility of delinquent involvements." Social Problems, 18(spring):522-535.
JOHNSTON, J.D., Jr., and KNAPP, C.L. (1971). "Sex discrimination by law: A study in judicial perspective." New York University Law Review, 46(October):675-747.
KITTRIE, N.N. (1971). The right to be different. Baltimore: Johns Hopkins University Press.

LADNER, J. (1971). Tomorrow's tomorrow. Garden City, N.Y.: Doubleday.

LANGLEY, M.H. (1972). "The juvenile court: The making of a delinquent." Law and Society Review, 7(winter):273-298.

LEFSTEIN, N., STAPLETON, V., and TEITELBAUM, L. (1969). "In search of juvenile justice—*Gault* and its implications." Law and Society Review, 3(May): 491-562.

LERMAN, P. (1971). "Child convicts." Transaction, 8(July/August):35-44, 72.

LIEBOW, E. (1967). Tally's Corner: A study of Negro streetcorner men. Boston: Little, Brown.

MACK, J.W. (1909). "The juvenile court." Harvard Law Review, 23:104-122.

MEAD, M. (1949). Male and female. New York: Dell.

MONAHAN, T.P. (1970). "Police dispositions of juvenile offenders." Phylon, 21(summer):129-141.

PILIAVIN, I., and BRIAR, S. (1964). "Police encounters with juveniles." American Journal of Sociology, 70(September):206-214.

PLATT, A.M. (1969). The child savers. Chicago: University of Chicago Press.

President's Commission on Law Enforcement and Administration of Justice (1967). Task Force report: Juvenile delinquency and youth crime. Washington, D.C.: U.S. Government Printing Office.

RAINWATER, L. (1966). "Crucible of identity: The Negro lower-class family." Daedalus, 95(winter):172-216.

——— (1970). Behind ghetto walls. Chicago: Aldine.

REISS, A.J. (1960). "Sex offenses: The marginal status of the adolescent." Law and Contemporary Problems, 25(spring):309-333.

TERRY, R.M. (1967). "Discrimination in the handling of juvenile offenders by social control agencies." Journal of Research in Crime and Delinquency, 4(July): 218-230.

VEDDER, C.B., and SOMERVILLER, D.B. (1970). The delinquent girl. Springfield, Ill.: Charles C Thomas.

Yale Law Journal (1973). Note, "*Parens patriae* and statutory vagueness in the juvenile court." 82(March):745-771.

L. Thomas Winfree, Jr.
East Texas State University

Curt T. Griffiths
Simon Fraser University

5

ADOLESCENT ATTITUDES
TOWARD THE POLICE
A Survey of High School Students

Among the factors considered crucial for good police public relations is the establishment and maintenance of a favorable public image. Prassel (1975:84) notes that while a majority of Americans are satisfied with the job the police are doing, community relations is a problem of considerable magnitude for law enforcement. Prassel contends that the sources of this apparent paradox are the groups most often associated with crime, which are, in his estimation, the young, poor, and minorities. "For the police, who sometimes appear to restrict rather than assist the public, the problem is essentially one of changing attitudes and images. The emphasis can be altered from repression to service and from fear to respect" (Prassel, 1975:85). Adams, Buck, and Hallstrom (1974:393) liken the public relations building process to that of any large business where an attempt is undertaken to "present their products or services in the best possible light."

It is interesting to note, but not entirely unexpected, that one of the "target groups" mentioned by Prassel and Adams et al., as well as other researchers and practitioners in the area of police science and administration (Hoobler, 1973; MacIver, 1966), is the youth of America. The establishment of a favorable image with this particular group in society is important because the policeman is often the first, and not infrequently the only, official of the criminal justice system with whom many juveniles come into contact (Cavan and Ferdinand, 1975:314). It has been suggested that each time the police officer has to deal with a child he "holds court" (Caldwell and Black, 1971:162). At that point an initial decision is made to release the adolescent with a warning or bring charges against him and perhaps even take the juvenile to the police station. Caldwell and Black (1971:161) report that about 75% of the delinquency cases appearing before juvenile courts are brought by police agencies. It is further estimated that approximately 45% of the juvenile offenders taken into custody are handled within the police department and released (Federal Bureau of Investigation, 1972).

It would appear, then, that these early contacts are very important in shaping future relationships between the youth and the criminal justice system. This research attempts to explore this important area of police-community relations by examining the following questions: (1) Are certain adolescents more likely to have negative contacts with the police than positive ones? and (2) What is the impact of these contacts, both positive and negative, on adolescent perceptions of the police?

RELATED RESEARCH

Many studies of police and juvenile relationships have examined the handling of the adolescents by police agencies (Wertham and Piliavin, 1967; Sellin and Wolfgang, 1964; Bordua, 1967; Wilson, 1968). Not infrequently, the research focuses on the use of discretion by police officers in the processing of juvenile offenders. In a study of attitudes expressed toward officers, Bordua (1967) found that petitions were filed more often in cases where the individual was evasive or antisocial than in cases where they were honest and responsive. In a similar vein, Piliavin and Briar (1964) found that youths who were uncooperative were more likely to be arrested and those adolescents who were cooperative were more likely to be admonished and released. Finally, it has also been established that the police may consider the offense, prior record of the offender, family record, and demeanor of the victim prior to and after a decision to arrest the offender (Sellin and Wolfgang, 1964).

Not uncommonly, however, the prior record of the offender, the family record or even the demeanor and attitude of the victim are unknown to the officer in the field. Some researchers have suggested that in instances where such information is unavailable, the actions of the police can only be described as prejudiced. For example, Piliavin and Briar (1964) note that black and male juveniles whose appearance matched a delinquent stereotype were stopped and interrogated more frequently than others. In addition, they were given more severe dispositions for the same offenses. This process of selective apprehension appeared to Piliavin and Briar (1964) to stem from two sources. First, the police, from experience, had reason to believe that these individuals were more "dangerous"; that the black males and "tough" looking whites tend to commit crimes more frequently than do other types of youths. Second, selective enforcement also results from long held prejudices on the part of individual police officers (Piliavin and Briar, 1964:211).

While the position that the police are prejudicial in their apprehension and detention practices seems to be supported by the statistics on arrest, especially for sex and race (Haskell and Yablonsky, 1974:67-75), other researchers have been skeptical of such charges (Terry, 1967a, 1967b; Black and Reiss, 1970; Weiner and Willie, 1971). By way of example, Terry (1967a, 1967b) found little support for the prejudicial treatment thesis at several different juvenile contact points with the criminal justice system. In his study of the screening of juvenile offenders, Terry (1967a) found that the severity of the sanctions accorded juvenile delinquents varied considerably from agency to agency, and the dispositions did not appear to be related to the power of the juveniles or their social distance from the police. In general, Terry (1967a, 1967b) found that minority status, socioeconomic status, and delinquency rates are relatively unimportant variables in the determination of a disposition at the arrest stage, probationary stage, or juvenile court stage.

It appears that the majority of the existing studies of police-adolescent relations have been concerned with what Prassel (1975) has termed the "restriction" and "repression" of adolescent activities. The examination of the positive consequences of the role of policemen has not been of a primary research concern. This does not mean, however, that the potential impact of "positive" or noncriminal contacts with police by adolescents has not been discussed. Cavan and Ferdinand (1975:326-327) include in their text on delinquency a section that explores the expansion of police functions in the area of preventive programs. MacIver (1966) also indicates that police should be more aware of alternatives open to them when dealing with troublesome children. He calls for the creation of a special bureau or police division to deal with the unique problems of juvenile delinquents; a proposal also advanced by Caldwell and Black (1971:167-170). MacIver (1966:147) recommended that

> Police on the beat should be carefully trained to show a friendly attitude to the public, especially in areas inhabited by minority or disprivileged groups. The exhibition of bias and intolerance or needless roughness not only alienates the community and discourages public cooperation, but also provokes hostile demonstrations and dangerous incidents. The police are the guardians of the people. That is the face they should show to the community.

Hoobler (1973) likewise expresses concern about the negative attitude of a large portion of the young toward officers in uniform. As a solution to this problem he proposes that police task forces visit secondary school campuses in an effort to present the police officer and his role to the adolescents in a primarily nonenforcement situation. In this manner, "students [would come] to see the uniformed officer in his enforcement role and accept that role as a very necessary part of the community" (Hoobler, 1973:30). Thus MacIver, Hoobler, and many other researchers and practitioners in the area of police-community relations are in general agreement that police can and must improve their image among adolescents. And at least one way to achieve this goal is by their increasing positive contacts with the young and by reducing both confrontations and general harassment of adolescents based on racial, ethnic, sexual, or socioeconomic characteristics.

THE PROBLEM

The preceding discussion suggests that certain adolescents are more likely than others to report experiencing negative versus positive contacts with police. In particular, a number of studies of police-juvenile relations suggest that the lower socioeconomic status, minority male is most likely to have contacts with police that involve primarily law enforcement practices. These individuals, conversely, are less likely to have contacts with the police that involve the nonlaw enforcement, helping, humanitarian services of the police. High socioeconomic status, nonminority females constitute the group least likely to have negative contacts with police and most likely to have positive contacts with police.

On the basis of these observations and the literature review, the following hypotheses are offered:

(1) Males have a higher portion of negative contacts with the police than females.

(2) Females have a higher portion of positive contacts with the police than males.

(3) Lower socioeconomic status adolescents have a higher portion of negative contacts with the police than higher socioeconomic status adolescents.

(4) Higher socioeconomic status adolescents have a higher portion of positive contacts with the police than lower socioeconomic status adolescents.

(5) Minority youth have a higher portion of negative contacts with the police than nonminority youth.

(6) Nonminority youth have a higher portion of positive contacts with the police than minority youth.

An additional factor not usually examined in police-adolescent relations involves the rural-urban pattern of contacts. Basically, we are asking: Do rural adolescents experience more positive or negative contacts with the police when compared to their urban counterparts? The literature on rural-urban differences and the police, such as it is, does not suggest the existence of any particular pattern. It is possible that there are not any differences between the nature of the contacts rural and urban adolescents report with the police. However, Griffiths and Hall (1973) note that the working climate of the rural police officer is considerably different than that of his urban colleague. In general, the rural police officer has more time to deal with each situation than the urban officer. There is less concern with getting to the next call. Also, the threat of personal violence from the public is less in the rural setting. Finally, the rural policeman is likely to know most if not all of the adolescents in his jurisdiction. Therefore, the need to stop and question "suspicious" adolescents is reduced, and along with it a major source of negative contacts with the young. All in all, the contacts of the rural police officer with civilians are probably of a more positive nature than those of the urban policeman.

Since the general contacts between adolescents and the urban police, as noted in the review of the literature, can best be characterized as negative, and since it would appear that the contacts of the rural adolescent with police officers may be of a more positive nature, the following hypotheses are offered:

(7) Urban adolescents have a higher portion of negative contacts with the police than rural adolescents.

(8) Rural adolescents have a higher portion of positive contacts with the police than urban adolescents.

The second major concern of this paper is to explore the relationship between contacts with the police and adolescent perceptions of law enforcement. We suggest that the type of contacts with police function as a mediating variable between the four individual characteristic factors and adolescent perceptions of the police. This observation is grounded in the studies which suggest that, due to negative contacts with police officers, the young, poor, and minorities see the police in an unfavorable light (Black and Reiss, 1970; Portune, 1967). Contacts, then, appear to mediate between these factors and adolescent perceptions of the police.

The following hypotheses are suggested:

(9) The greater the negative contacts with the police, the more negative the attitude toward the police.

(10) The greater the positive contacts with the police, the more positive the attitude toward the police.

Finally, the discussions presented by Hoobler (1973) and MacIver (1966) concerning police-adolescent relations suggest one final factor for the analysis. That is, the police community programs in the high schools appear to be designed to increase the student's understanding of the police officer's job and to improve his evaluation of the police. However, we propose that just as negative contacts may influence the adolescent's attitudes toward the police, these same contacts influence as well adolescent prestige ratings of the police.

The relationships discussed above are expressed in the following hypotheses:

(11) The greater the negative contacts with the police, the more negative the prestige ratings of the police officer's job.

(12) The greater the positive contacts with the police, the more positive the prestige rating of the police officer's job.

(13) The greater the prestige rating of the police officer's job, the more positive the attitude toward the police.

In summary, the hypothesized relationships expressed in the preceding discussion propose that certain adolescents are likely to report more negative than positive contacts with the police. In particular, lower socioeconomic status, maleness, minority status, and urban residence pattern are related to a high incidence of negative contacts and a low incidence of positive contacts. Conversely, high socioeconomic status, nonminority status, femaleness, and rural residence pattern are related to low incidence of negative contacts with high incidence of positive contacts. Finally, these contacts are thought of as influencing both prestige ratings and attitudes toward the police, with the ratings also being directly related to adolescent attitudes.

METHODOLOGY

The Data

During the spring of 1974, a questionnaire was administered to high school students residing in selected rural and urban areas. More specifically, five schools, in each of the following cities, were randomly selected from *Patterson's American Education* (1974): (1) Seattle, (2) Portland, (3) San Francisco, (4) Los Angeles, and (5) San Diego. For the rural sample, 10 high schools in the western portion of a rural western state were selected. In addition, the rural sample included the boy's state training school, the girl's state institution, and a youth work camp. Inclusion of these latter institutions allowed the administration of the questionnaire to youths with extensive contacts with law enforcement. The total number of schools selected for the study was 38.

In the urban portion of the schools contacted, 18 of 25 schools returned the inquiry cards, and seven agreed to participate. Positive reply cards were received from 10 of the 13 rural schools initially contacted, including two of the three state institutions. From the 17 participating schools, a total of 869 questionnaires were obtained. Approximately one-half of the total sample was urban and the other half rural.

The Analysis Design

Multiple regression and path analysis are our basic analytic techniques. The coefficients reported in this report are the net standardized effects or beta coefficients. Patterns of indirect effects, both causal and noncausal, are computed through the standard "tracing" rules of path analysis. The techniques and assumptions of path analysis are available in a number of sources (Duncan, 1966; Heise, 1969; Land, 1969; Nygreen,

1971) and need not be recapitulated here. Also, excellent discussions of direct and indirect effects are available in the works of Finney (1972) and Smith (1972, 1974).

One final note about the data is in order. Several of the variables operationalized in the following section are nominal and ordinal at best. In the case of nominal level data, dummy coding is used. That is, in the case of dichotomous nominal variables, the respondent either exhibits or does not exhibit that particular characteristic. The ordinal variables are handled in a slightly different manner. That is, following the lead of Bohrnstedt and Carter (1971) and Labovitz (1970), we will treat the ordinal variables as if they had equal intervals. This practice is justified by the observation that the robustness of regression analysis offsets any errors made by assuming such intervals. Or as Labovitz (1970:515) states:

> Although some small error may accompany the treatment of ordinal variables as if they were interval, this is offset by the use of the more powerful, more sensitive, better developed and more clearly interpretable statistic with known sampling error.

VARIABLES AND INDICATORS

Exogenous Variables

The four independent or exogenous variables suggested by the review of relevant literature are socioeconomic status, sex, residence pattern, and minority status. The total variation of these predetermined variables is assumed to be explained by variables outside of those under consideration (Land, 1969:6).

Socioeconomic status. The socioeconomic status of the respondents was obtained by asking them their father's occupations, requesting that they be as specific as possible. This information was then coded into Duncan's (1961) nine item population decile.

Sex. The sex of the respondents was dummy coded into presence or absence of male sex. In the sample there were 391 females (45%) and 478 males (55%).

Residence pattern. As previously mentioned, the high school students who constituted the sample attended school in 17 different school districts in four states. Seven of the schools were located in urban centers, while the remaining 10 were in rural areas. Again, this variable was dummy coded into presence or absence of urban residence pattern. Urban adolescents accounted for just under half of the total sample.

Minority status. We asked each respondent his or her ethnic background. They could choose from the following categories: (1) Black, (2) Native American, (3) White/Anglo, (4) Chicano, (5) Oriental, and (6) others. This information was coded into a dichotomy of minority/nonminority adolescents. This variable was also dummy coded for the regression analysis.

Endogenous Variables

Contained within the hypotheses derived from the literature review are several endogenous variables, or variables in which the total variation is "assumed to be completely determined by some linear combination of variables in the system" (Land, 1969:6). An endogenous variable can be dependent upon other endogenous variables, exogenous variables, or combinations of exogenous and endogenous variables. However, all endogenous variables are ultimately determined by the exogenous variables (Land, 1969:6). The endogenous variables present within the current research are positive contacts, negative contacts, and prestige ratings of the police officer's job.

Contacts with the police. The contacts with the police were self-reported. They consisted of two general types: (1) positive contacts and (2) negative contacts. Negative contacts involved such things as having been stopped by the police, having had a close friend or relative arrested by the police, and having been arrested themselves by the police. The possible responses to these questions were "yes" and "no." Those juveniles answering "yes" to all three inquiries were conceived of as being high on negative contacts with the police; those with some "yes" answers or all "no" responses had had negative contacts with the police to a lesser degree. The indicator of positive police contacts was constructed in a similar manner. That is, the adolescents were asked whether any of their close friends or relatives were policemen, whether they knew any policemen personally, and whether they or a member of their family had ever called the police for assistance.

Prestige rating of police officer's job. There are many techniques for measuring the prestige associated with an occupation. For the current research and target population, we selected the simplest technique. That is, we simply asked each respondent to rate the prestige associated with the policeman's job as (1) high, (2) medium, or (3) low.

Dependent Variable

Adolescent attitudes toward the police. A 16 item Likert scale developed by Griffiths (1974) was used to measure the dependent variable of the attitudes expressed by high school students toward the police. All items used in the scale were found to be significant at least at the .001 level in item to scale tests. The scale obtained a split-half reliability coefficient of .89 that was raised by the Spearman-Brown formula to .94. There were eight positive items and eight negative items. Six Likert-type response categories were used. There was not a "Don't know" or "Neither" response category. The scale was coded so that the higher the score on the summated score, the more positive the attitude toward the police. Sample items include the following: "I trust policemen," "I feel policemen are easy to get along with," "Policemen use their badges as an excuse to rough up people," and "Policemen like to hassle young people."

FINDINGS

The product-moment coefficients of correlation between the eight variables critical to this report are presented in Table 1. With three exceptions, the bivariate associations reported in this table are negligible to low. The first exception involves the negative contacts with the police (N) and attitude toward the police (A). In this case the association is inverse and moderately low ($r_{AN} = -.28$). In other words, juveniles who have negative contacts with the police do indeed tend to have more negative attitudes toward the police.

Table 1: CORRELATION AND STANDARDIZED PATH COEFFICIENTS FOR TOTAL MODEL[a]

	X	L	S	M	P	N	R	A
Sex (X)	1.00	.17 —	.00 —	.08 —	.02 (.02)	.31 (.32)	−.11 (−.12)	−.10 (.02)
Residence pattern (L)		1.00	.02 —	−.06 —	.02 (.02)	−.01 (−.07)	.06 (.06)	.05 (.02)
Socioeconomic status (S)			1.00	−.13 —	.01 (.00)	−.01 (−.01)	.03 (.03)	.09 (.05)
Minority status (M)				1.00	−.03 (−.03)	.01 (.01)	−.02 (−.01)	−.13 (−.12)
Positive contacts (P)					1.00	.14 (.14)	.10 (.12)	.14 (.15)
Negative contacts (N)						1.00	−.11 (−.13)	−.28 (−.27)
Prestige ratings (R)							1.00	.33 (.29)
Attitude toward police (A)								1.00

a. The standardized path coefficients are presented in the parentheses throughout the table.

The second exception is the association between adolescent ratings of police prestige (R) and their attitudes toward the police (A). In this instance, the correlation reported is positive and moderately low (r_{AR} = .33). Again, juveniles who rated the prestige of the policeman's job highly tended to have more positive attitudes toward the police. The final exception involves the sex of the respondent (X) and the amount of negative contacts (N). The relationship is in the predicted direction; that is, maleness is associated with negative contacts with the police, and moderately low (r_{NX} = .31).

Outside of these three exceptions, then, the largest theoretically important bivariate association reported in Table 1 is between positive contacts with the police (P) and attitudes toward the police (A), in which case the simple r value was equal to .14. However, the rest of the bivariate associations are in the predicted directions, albeit small. Clearly, the bivariate analysis of the correlation coefficients provides us with no defensible criteria for rejecting or accepting the relationships proposed between the variables other than the relative size of the coefficient. For a better idea of the relative directness or indirectness of the effects of the endogenous and exogenous variables on the dependent variable of attitude toward the police regardless of the size of the bivariate intercorrelations, we will use the path analytic technique (Duncan, 1966; Land, 1969).

Figure 1 is a representation of the path model implied in our earlier discussion. Included in this representation are all possible paths. However, following Heise's (1969) suggestion that models be as parsimonious as possible and Land's (1969) contention that one must establish a rejection level for unacceptable paths, several of the proposed paths have been eliminated and are represented by broken lines. We adopted the .05 level as the rejection level. That is, any path that failed to achieve a value of greater than .05 was rejected.

While the amount of variance explained in the dependent variable by the four exogenous variables and three endogenous variables is 22%, this model may not be the most parsimonious path model. This speculation is based on several observations.

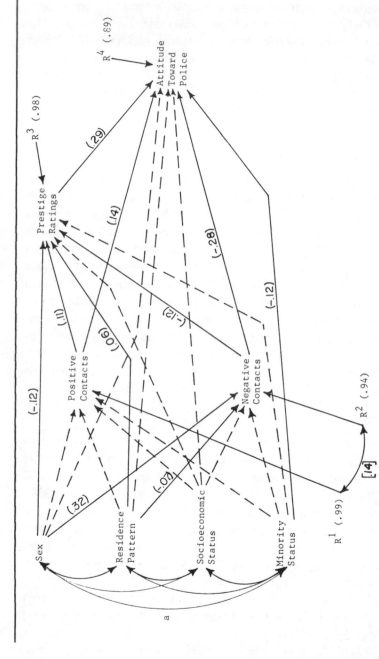

a. The intercorrelations between the exogenous variables and the path coefficients for the broken-line paths, which represent non-significant paths, are contained in Table 1.

Figure 1. PATH MODEL FOR THE DETERMINANTS OF ADOLESCENT ATTITUDES TOWARD THE POLICE

First, the amount of unexplained variance in both the negative and positive contacts with the police is relatively high. In fact, the four exogenous variables contribute virtually nothing to the explanation of the positive contacts, as witnessed by the lack of a single path to survive the size criterion. Only two of the exogenous variables—sex (X) and residence pattern (L)—exhibited resistant paths with negative contacts. In this instance, the amount of variance left unexplained was less than that for positive contacts (98% versus 88%). Second, the residual covariation between positive contacts (P) and negative contacts (N) is virtually identical to the bivariate correlation between these two variables. That is, the correlation coefficient that results from controlling for the exogenous variables in the relationship between positive and negative contacts (r = .139) is almost identical to the zero-order correlation between these two variables (r = .143). Finally, only five of the 16 possible paths between the four exogenous variables and the other four variables in the model even marginally survived the size criterion.

The concern of this paper is the explanation of adolescent attitudes toward the police. We are interested in developing the most parsimonious model for this task. If the amount of unexplained variance is greatly increased by removing sex, residence pattern, socioeconomic status, and minority status from the path model, then perhaps they are critical. On the other hand, if the unexplained variance is not greatly increased, and the number of independent variables is reduced, our model may be enhanced by adopting a strategy of "model trimming" (Heise, 1969). It should not be overlooked that by trimming these particular variables from our model we are implying that the sex, residence pattern, socioeconomic status, and minority status of the adolescents explain very little about not only their attitudes toward the police, but also the number and type of contacts adolescents have with the police and their ratings of the prestige of the policeman's job.

The amount of variance explained in the more parsimonious model, Figure 2, is approximately the same as in the eight variable models previously examined. Specifically, 20% of the variance in the dependent variable is explained by the three variables of positive police contacts, negative police contacts, and prestige ratings. This means, conversely, that the four exogenous variables were explaining approximately 2% of the variance in the dependent variable. Since we can explain virtually the same amount of variance in the dependent variable without these four variables, it appears they are not critical to the model.

The path analytic technique mandates an examination of the indirect as well as direct causal effects. We are concerned with the amount of correlation that is the result of indirect paths through other variables. In the model presented in Figure 2, we might wish to know how much of the covariance between negative contacts (N) and attitudes (A) is "interpreted" by prestige ratings (R). Similarly, we might wish to know how much of the covariance between the positive contacts (P) and attitudes (A) is mediated through the same endogenous variable. Conversely, the relationships between positive contacts (P) and prestige ratings, negative contacts (N) and prestige ratings (R), prestige ratings (R) and attitudes (A) are all taken as genuine and direct (Finney, 1972:175-185; Nie et al., 1975:388). In these latter cases, there are no variables intervening between the causal and effects variables.

Using the technique proposed by Finney (1972:175-186), we decomposed the relationship in the revised model. The results

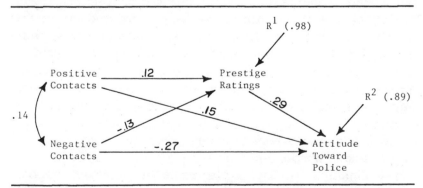

Figure 2. REVISED PATH MODEL: DIFFERENTIAL CONTACTS, PRESTIGE RATINGS AND ATTITUDES TOWARD THE POLICE

of this decomposition process are presented in Table 2. In the bivariate relationships between positive contacts and prestige ratings, negative contacts and prestige ratings, and prestige ratings and attitudes the effects are, as discussed above, all direct. Also, the sum of the unanalyzed effects in each of these relationships is slight (—.02 for the prestige ratings and positive contacts; .02 for the prestige ratings and negative contacts; .04 for the attitude toward the police and prestige ratings). However, between both sets of contacts and attitudes there are indirect effects. Likewise, some small part of these relationships is, as shown in Table 2, spurious. Due to the relatively small size of the indirect effects and the similarity between the total covariance and the direct causal effects in both instances, the amount of spuriousness found was minimal (—.04 and .03 for the bivariate relationships between attitudes and positive contacts and attitudes and negative contacts respectively). No revisions in the model are required.

DISCUSSION AND CONCLUSIONS

This research was designed to explore juvenile attitudes toward the police. We found that the sex, socioeconomic status, residence pattern, and minority status of the adolescent have little effect upon the relationship between their contacts with the police, their prestige ratings of the policeman's job or their attitudes toward the police. Positive and negative contacts with the police and the prestige ratings themselves, however, appear to be fairly critical in shaping adolescent attitudes toward the police. In fact, the elimination of the variables of sex, minority status, residence pattern, and socioeconomic status from our model barely decreases the amount of variance explained in the dependent variable. Consequently, we revised the model as suggested by the model trimming section of the analysis and eliminated these variables from the model.

An examination of the revised model reveals several additional findings. The positive and negative contacts are only weakly associated. It would appear that having negative contacts with the police does not preclude one from having

Table 2: REVISED PATH MODEL: A SUMMARY OF THE DIRECT EFFECTS, TOTAL INDIRECT EFFECTS, AND UNANALYZED COMPONENTS

Endogenous Variables	Exogenous Variables	Direct Effect	Sum of Indirect Effects	Total Causal Impact	Sum of Unanalyzed Components	Sum of Effects	Zero-Orders	Discrepancy[a]
Prestige ratings $R^2 = .04$	Positive contacts	.12	--	.12	-.02	.10	.10	.00
	Negative contacts	-.13	--	-.13	.02	-.11	-.11	.00
Attitude toward police $R^2 = .20$	Positive contacts	.15	.03	.18	-.04	.14	.14	.00
	Negative contacts	-.27	-.04	-.31	.03	-.28	-.28	.00
	Prestige ratings	.29	--	.29	.04	.33	.33	.00

a. The observed zero-order Pearson Product-Moment correlation minus the Sum of Effects. The sign of the discrepancy value is an indication as to whether the zero-order correlation is an overestimation (+) or an underestimation (−) of the effects.

positive contacts. Second, the prestige ratings, while exhibiting the strongest path with attitudes toward the police, are virtually unexplained by the contact variables. Only 4% of the variance in the prestige rating variable is accounted for by the positive and negative contacts with the police.

The final finding is perhaps the most intriguing since it is also the most difficult to interpret. The finding itself is fairly straightforward. The path between negative police contacts reported and attitudes is nearly twice the size as that for positive police contacts and attitudes (−.27 versus .15). It appears that negative contacts with the police, regardless of their origin, are almost twice as important in determining juvenile attitudes toward the police as positive contacts.

There are several possible interpretations of this finding. Perhaps the one most cogent to this paper is that, while a preponderance of positive contacts may result in positive attitudes toward the police, negative contacts carry more "weight." That is, even in the face of positive contacts, negative ones could result in lower attitudes toward the police. Therefore, if the police intend to promote good public relations with adolescents, and at the same time stimulate positive attitudes toward the police in this group, they should avoid negative contacts, while increasing positive ones. Unfortunately, even this "solution" is problematic since our findings suggest that negative contacts are more damaging to the creation of positive attitudes than positive contacts are helpful.

Our findings, with respect to adolescent attitudes toward the police, are not conclusive. Nonetheless, in our study, police contacts, both positive and negative, are not associated with sex, race, residence, or socioeconomic status. Likewise, neither are the adolescent ratings of the police or attitudes toward the police associated with these variables. The analysis revealed that a considerable amount of adolescent attitudes toward the police is explained by contacts with and prestige ratings of law enforcement officers. The negative contacts are approximately twice as important in the determination of juvenile attitudes toward police officers as positive ones, with the prestige ratings contributing nearly the same explanatory force as the negative contacts.

In conclusion, these findings suggest that a possible approach for the police to pursue is the one mentioned by Hoobler (1973), MacIver (1966), and others. That is, positive contacts with the public in general and the young in particular should be maximized. In this manner, perhaps the police can improve their public image. However, two final points should be considered as potential problems that might plague the implementors of such an approach. First, maximizing positive contacts while minimizing negative ones may be seen by the officer in the field as a difficult if not impossible task to accomplish without interfering with the enforcement of the law and the maintenance of order. Second, it should be understood that the gains made by positive contacts may be completely offset by negative ones.

REFERENCES

ADAMS, T.F., BUCK, G., and HALLSTROM, D. (1974). Criminal justice organization and management. Pacific Palisades, Calif.: Goodyear.

BLACK, D.J., and REISS, A.J. (1970). "Police control of juveniles." American Sociological Review, 35:63-77.

BOHRNSTEDT, G.W., and CARTER, L.F. (1971). "Robustness in regression analysis." Chapter 5 in H.L. Costner (ed.), Sociological methodology: 1971. San Francisco: Jossey-Bass.

BORDUA, D.J. (1967). "Recent trends: Deviant behavior and social control." Annals of the American Academy of Political and Social Sciences, 359:159-161.

CALDWELL, R.G., and BLACK, J.A. (1971). Juvenile delinquency. New York: Ronald Press.

CAVAN, R.C., and FERDINAND, T.N. (1975). Juvenile delinquency. Philadelphia: J.B. Lippincott.

DUNCAN, O.D. (1961). "A socioeconomic index for all occupations." Pp. 109-138 in A.G. Reiss, Jr. (ed.), Occupations and social status. New York: Free Press.

——— (1966). "Path analysis: Sociological examples." American Journal of Sociology, 72:1-16.

ELLIOT, N.F. (ed., 1974). Patterson's American education. Mount Prospect, Ill.: Educational Directories.

Federal Bureau of Investigation (1972). Uniform Crime Reports, Crime in the United States. Washington, D.C.: U.S. Government Printing Office.

FINNEY, J.M. (1972). "Indirect effects in path analysis." Sociological Methods and Research, 1:175-186.

GRIFFITHS, C.T. (1974). "The construction of an instrument for measuring adolescent attitudes toward the police." Unpublished paper.

GRIFFITHS, C.T., and HALL, E.L. (1973). "Social isolation among rural sheriffs' deputies." Unpublished paper.

HASKELL, M.R., and YABLONSKY, L. (1974). Juvenile delinquency. Chicago: Rand McNally.

HEISE, D.R. (1969). "Problems in path analysis and causal inferences." Pp. 38-73 in E.F. Borgatta (ed.), Sociological methodology: 1969. San Francisco: Jossey-Bass.

HOOBLER, R.L. (1973). "San Diego: Secondary schools' task force." Police Chief, 40:28-30.

LABOVITZ, S. (1970). "The assignment of numbers to rank-order categories." American Sociological Review, 35:515-525.

LAND, K.C. (1969). "Principles of path analysis." Pp. 3-37 in E.F. Borgatta (ed.), Sociological methodology: 1969. San Francisco: Jossey-Bass.

MacIVER, R.M. (1966). The prevention and control of delinquency. New York: Atherton.

NIE, N.C., JENKINS, J.G., STEINBRENNER, K., and BENT, D.H. (1975). SPSS: Statistical package for the social sciences. New York: McGraw Hill.

NYGREEN, G.T. (1971). "Interactive path analysis." American Sociologist, 6:37-43.

PILIAVIN, I., and BRIAR, S. (1964). "Police encounters with juveniles." American Journal of Sociology, 70:206-214.

PORTUNE, R. (1967). Cincinnati Police-Juvenile Attitude Project: A demonstration in police-teacher curriculum development. Washington, D.C.: U.S. Department of Justice.

PRASSEL, F.R. (1975). Introduction to American criminal justice. New York: Harper and Row.

SELLIN, T., and WOLFGANG, M.E. (1964). The measurement of delinquency. New York: John Wiley.

SMITH, R.B. (1972). "Neighborhood context and college plans: An ordinal path analysis." Social Forces, 51:199-217.

——— (1974). "Continuities in ordinal path analysis." Social Forces, 53:200-229.

TERRY, R.M. (1967a). "The screening of juvenile offenders." Journal of Criminal Law, Criminology and Police Science, 58:173-181.

——— (1967b). "Discrimination in the handling of juvenile offenders by social control agencies." Journal of Research in Crime and Delinquency, 4:218-230.

WEINER, N.L., and WILLIE, C.V. (1971). "Decisions by juvenile officers." American Journal of Sociology, 77:199-210.

WERTHAM, C., and PILIAVIN, I. (1967). "Gang members and the police." Pp. 56-78 in D.L. Bordua (ed.), The police. New York: John Wiley.

WILSON, J.Q. (1968). "The police and the delinquent in two cities." Pp. 9-30 in S. Wheeler (ed.), Controlling delinquents. New York: John Wiley.

Richard A. Ball
West Virginia University

6

EMERGENT DELINQUENCY IN
A RURBAN AREA

Delinquency research in the United States focused largely on the behavior of males in large cities. This double bias has become even more serious with the rapid increase in delinquency among girls and given the fact that more than one-half of the population of the United States resides either in rural areas or in small cities of between 2,500 or 50,000 population. In view of the considerable problems associated with the concepts "rural" and "urban," particularly those having to do with the multidimensionality issue, the ecological range will be referred to as a rural-urban "concatenation," by which is meant only a unified series. The present research was designed partly in an effort to explore one complex portion of that concatenation, a type of area which might have been designated as "hinterland" (Gibbons, 1972) or simply "nonmetropolitan" (Polk, 1967), which will be designated here by the older and more specific term, "rurban."[1]

The rural-urban concatenation may be defined in terms of the complementary principles of gradience and differentiation. According to the gradient principle, the extent of urban influence varies directly with the proximity and size of the nearest city (Martin, 1957:176). The principle of differentiation amounts to a modification stating that urban influence also varies directly with the extent to which an area is ecologically differentiated by specialization and functional interdependency of the ecological components within the particular area (Martin, 1957:176). Thus, the sort of area with which we are concerned combines certain characteristics associated with both the rural and urban extremes.

Rather than generalize about "delinquency," this study will focus upon the particular phase of delinquency *emergence* defined in terms of "basic norm violation." Basic norm violation is behavior contrary to the *fundamental* normative restrictions placed on youth with respect to driving, drinking, theft, vandalism, truancy, parental defiance, and sexual behavior. Although one may argue over the "seriousness" of these activities, there is little question that they represent violation of the *basic* normative restrictions which collectively define the status of youth. The Nye-Short Scale offers a measure of basic norm violation.[2]

While there are obviously important differences among various ecological areas which might be termed "rurban," Marion County, West Virginia, offers a reasonable example of such a context. Marion County is located approximately two hours driving time from Pittsburgh and is composed of a small central city of 29,000 population surrounded by small towns (most of which have populations of less than 2,500) interspersed through a satellite fringe area of essentially nonfarm character. The county is an economically differentiated area producing coke, coal, tar, cement products, clay products, powder, lumber, pumps, chemicals, foundry products, aluminum products, glass, glassware, flourescent lamps, chemical foundry products, corrugated boxes, machinery, electronic parts, novelties, and other products (Lilly, 1969:58-66). The population is essentially working class, with only 34.6% of the work force in white-collar occupations.

The area has a population density of 197.3 per square mile, with 54% of the 61,356 residents living in areas which the census designates as "rural" and 46% residing in "urban" areas. Data were gathered on 96.5% of the sixth graders enrolled in the 41 public elementary schools of Marion County with analysis confined to subsamples of 398 males and 407 females, all of whom were white working-class youth. Working class was defined by a score of 70 or below on an interpolated North-Hatt Scale as described by Kahl (1957).

Selection of independent variables is guided by the "containment theory" developed by Reckless (1967:469-483), a framework which is particularly useful for present purposes. Containment theory is applicable to both male and female offenses and to different age levels. Moreover, it represents a specific attempt to relate attitudinal variables to ecological context, arguing that certain specified "self-factors" comprise an "inner containment" which, along with various environmental factors that together comprise an "outer containment," seriously affect the risk of delinquent or criminal behavior. Having specified the "outer" context in terms of such structural variables as social class, age, sex, and ecological area, this research will focus upon three major social psychological or "self" factors which may be derived as independent variables within the general framework—*norm neutralization, anomia,* and *self-concept.*[3]

Norm Neutralization

According to the "neutralization theory" proposed by Sykes and Matza (1957), delinquency represents the behavior of fairly conventional individuals who apply to their actions culturally available excuses which serve as "techniques" to "neutralize" the cultural norms in given situations. Specifically, Sykes and Matza assert that these "techniques of neutralization" include: (1) denial of responsibility, (2) denial of injury, (3) denial of the victim, (4) condemnation of the condemners, and (5) appeal to higher loyalties. Since there is reason to suspect that delinquency outside large cities involves "troublemaking" (Polk, 1967:346) and "norm erosion" (Reckless and Shoham, 1963) rather than a developed system of delinquent norms, and, since norm neutralization is probably a factor in norm erosion (Ball, 1966), neutralization may be a particularly relevant factor in the norm violations of rurban youth.

Since the earliest statement of the neutralization hypothesis, Matza (1964) has offered a modification, arguing that delinquency may be *less the result of personal neutralization than of the misperception of peer group attitudes.* If this is true, it implies that relatively few delinquents accept the norm neutralizing excuses themselves, but that they *act* as if they do, each believing that his peers accept them and being unwilling to admit that he does not. We can specify this process in terms of attribution theory (Triandis and Davis, 1965; Stephen, 1973), designating it as *attributed neutralization.* Neutralization was measured by the Abridged Neutralization Inventory with a corresponding Attributed Neutralization Inventory for measurement of the boys' perception of friends' attitudes.[4] If we formalize the argument, three distinct hypotheses emerge. (1) *Rurban sixth graders will tend to attribute significantly more neutralization to their friends than they report for themselves.* (2) *The attributions will significantly overestimate the neutralization which actually exists among these friends.* (3) *Attributed neutralization among rurban sixth graders will be related to basic norm violation at a higher level of confidence than will personal neutralization.*

Anomia

Most of the previous research dealing with anomia has been based upon the Srole Scale (Clinard, 1964). Srole (1956) describes the "anomic" person as one who feels that (1) social leaders are indifferent to his problems, (2) there is little chance for accomplishment in what is essentially an unpredictable society, (3) goals are receding from him, (4) no one can really be counted on to support him, and (5) life itself is meaningless and futile. Since the Srole Scale is aimed at the adult level of perception, a Juvenile Anomia Index was developed for use with the Srole Scale as another measure of generalized anomia.[5]

Adolescents, however, are not yet full participants in society, their contact being mediated by such proximate social systems as family and school (Jarrett and Haller, 1964; Stinchcombe, 1964), both of which have been identified as delinquency factors. Thus, it may be that anomia will exist in specific as well as generalized form and that certain specific forms may be more clearly related to delinquency than is general anomia. This possibility was pursued by use of a Family Anomia Index and a School Anomia Index.[6] The four distinct but related hypotheses lead us to expect that *basic norm violation among rurban sixth graders will be significantly and positively related to (1) Srole Scale scores, (2) juvenile anomia scores, (3) family anomia scores, and (4) school anomia scores.*

Self-Concept

The containment theory, along with a well-known series of studies by Reckless, Dinitz, and various associates (Reckless, Dinitz, and Murray, 1956, 1957; Reckless, Dinitz, and Kay, 1957; Dinitz, Reckless, and Kay, 1958; Scarpitti, Murray, Dinitz, and Reckless, 1960; Dinitz, Scarpitti, and Reckless, 1962; Reckless and Dinitz, 1967), also suggests that the self-concept factor may be of particular relevance to emergent delinquency in a rurban area. The central conclusion there is that the "good boy" who avoids difficulty with the law in spite of an ecological context of high delinquency risk does so as a result of a "favorable" self-concept which provides "insulation." Since criticism of this research has centered upon the definition of self-concept implied by the items in the Self-Concept Inventory (Schwartz and Tangri, 1965; Tangri and Schwartz, 1967; Hirschi and Selvin, 1967; Orcutt, 1970), some clarification is necessary. Although the critics recognize that the inventory is specifically defined as a measure of "the boy's perception of himself in reference to significant others in his immediate world" (Jensen, 1970:85), they fail to appreciate the meaning of such a definition. The concern is certainly *not* with self-esteem, as Tangri and Schwartz (1967) argue, nor is it a question of whether one "evaluates himself as a delinquent" (Jensen, 1970:88). Both the phrase, "in reference to significant others," and an examination of the items comprising the inventory make it clear that the inventory essentially represents one's *judgment* as to how he is perceived by "parents," "friends," "teachers," and "grown-ups," his *interpretation* of their behavior toward him, and his *prediction* of their future reaction to his behavior. Thus, the focus is upon the *attribution* phase of self-concept formation, a phase which may turn out to be more important than the internalization phase which is usually regarded as the final product. Using the Self-Concept Inventory as we have interpreted it above, our basic hypothesis is that a *significant positive relationship will exist between "unfavorable" self-concept scores and basic norm violation scores among rurban sixth graders.*

FINDINGS

Table 1 shows the pattern of basic norm violations for both males and females. With respect to the most common norm violation, "defying parents' authority to their face," there is no difference between the boys and the girls. All of the other percentage differences are statistically significant (P < .001), with boys reporting more basic norm violation in every case. The greatest differences appear for drinking violations and driving offenses.

Means on the abridged Nye-Short Scale are shown in Table 2, along with mean scores for two samples drawn from our earlier research (Ball, 1966).[7] The first is a sample of 125 white 15-year-old males from one of the same high delinquency urban areas studied by Reckless and his associates. The second is a sample of 115 white 15-18-year-old males from Ohio's institution for male juvenile delinquents. The mean score was significantly higher (P < .01) for the rurban boys than for the rurban girls. Mean scores for both the boys and the girls were significantly lower (P < .01) than those obtained for the samples from the high delinquency area and the institution for delinquents.

Mean personal neutralization scores are also shown in Table 2. Although the mean was somewhat higher for the boys than for the girls, the difference did not reach statistical significance. Nor were there significant differences between the mean personal neutralization scores of these rurban sixth graders and the mean obtained for the institutionalized delinquents. These means were, however, significantly *higher* (P < .001) than that obtained for the earlier sample of boys from a high delinquency urban area. As Table 3 indicates, the hypothesis of a significant

Table 1: PERCENTAGE OF RURBAN, WHITE, WORKING CLASS SIXTH GRADERS
REPORTING BASIC NORM VIOLATIONS, WITH 398 BOYS COMPARED
TO 407 GIRLS*

	Sex	
Basic Norm Violation	Boys	Girls
Defying parents authority to their face	50	50
Bought or drunk beer, wine, or liquor (including drinking at home)	35	15
Driving a car without a license or permit	33	15
Taking things that did not belong to them	25	15
Damaging or destroying property	25	15
Skipping school without a legitimate excuse	20	10

*Percentages rounded to nearest whole number.

positive relationship between personal neutralization and basic norm violation was supported for the boys only.

There were, however, certain patterns within the data which suggested the need for further analysis. First, the zero-order correlation, although statistically significant, was not particularly pronounced. Second, every independent variable tested, with the exception of Srole anomia, showed statistical significance, and Table 3 indicates that the zero-order correlations for these variables were essentially equal to or greater than that which obtained between personal neutralization and basic norm violation. Furthermore, the intercorrelations shown in Table 4 are generally significant, indicating that these variables are not independent of one another. All of this suggests that the apparent correlation between personal neutralization and basic norm violation may be accounted for by other variables.

It may be that self-concept is a variable that should be taken into account here. Containment theory indicates that self-concept is the key factor which may either "insulate" one from the effects of deviant pressures or open the way for these pressures, and this proposition has been supported by research. Table 3 shows that the self-concept was more clearly related to basic norm violation than any of the other independent variables employed. And, indeed, Table 5 does show that the relationship between norm neutralization and basic norm violation declines to statistical insignificance (τ xy.z = .04, P > .05) when self-concept is held constant.[8]

Table 2: MEAN NEUTRALIZATION, ANOMIA, SELF-CONCEPT, AND BASIC NORM VIOLATION SCORES FOR FOUR SAMPLES OF WHITE WORKING-CLASS YOUTH

	Variable							
	Neutralization			Anomia			Self-Concept Attitudes	Norm Basic Violation
Sample	Personal	Attributed	Srole	Juvenile	Family	School		
Institutionalized delinquents								
Boys (N = 125)	26.1	*	17.8	*	*	*	*	12.8
Urban high school								
Boys (N = 125)	20.1	*	15.4	*	*	*	*	6.9
Rurban elementary school								
Boys (N = 398)	27.0	29.9	16.4	16.7	19.5	23.9	4.7	4.2
Rurban elementary school								
Girls (N = 407)	25.1	28.7	15.2	16.7	19.6	22.9	3.6	2.9

*Unavailable

Table 3: VARIABLES RELATED TO BASIC NORM VIOLATION AMONG
RURBAN, WHITE, WORKING-CLASS SIXTH GRADERS,
WITH 398 BOYS COMPARED TO 407 GIRLS

Sex	Independent Variable	Correlation	Probability
Boys	Personal neutralization	.09	P < .05
	Attributed neutralization	.15	P < .001
	Srole scale	.04	P > .05
	Juvenile anomia	.09	P < .05
	Family anomia	.13	P < .001
	School anomia	.08	P < .05
	Self-concept	.28	P < .001
Girls	Personal neutralization	−.01	P > .05
	Attributed neutralization	.00	P > .05
	Srole scale	.08	P < .05
	Juvenile anomia	.11	P < .001
	Family anomia	.15	P < .001
	School anomia	.16	P < .001
	Self-concept	.28	P < .001

Our theoretical framework also suggests the need to control for the effects of attributed neutralization. Furthermore, from Tables 3 and 4 we see that the zero-order correlations between attributed neutralization scores and basic norm violation scores were exceeded only by those obtained for self-concept and that there was a pronounced relationship between scores on the Attributed Neutralization Inventory and those on the Personal Neutralization Inventory. The possibility is confirmed; Table 5 indicates that the correlation between personal neutralization and basic norm violation does decline to statistical insignificance (τ xy.z = .02, P > .05) when we control for the effect of attributed neutralization. As Table 5 indicates, none of the remaining variables has an appreciable effect upon the zero-order correlation.

Mean attributed neutralization scores are shown in Table 2. Again there was no significant difference between the mean scores of the boys and the girls. The means in both cases were significantly higher (P < .001) than those obtained for personal neutralization, supporting the hypothesis that rurban sixth graders will tend to attribute significantly more neutralization to their friends than they report for themselves. If it can be

Table 4: INTERCORRELATIONS AMONG INDEPENDENT VARIABLES FOR 398 MALE AND 407 FEMALE RURBAN, WHITE, WORKING-CLASS SIXTH GRADERS

First Independent Variable	Second Independent Variable											
	Attributed Neutralization		Anomia		Juvenile Anomia		Family Anomia		School Anomia		Self-Concept	
	Boys	Girls	Boys	Girls	Boys	Girls	Boys	Girls	Boys	Girls	Boys	Girls
Personal neutralization	.46	.48	.12	.20	.11	.19	.13	.13	.13	.13	.15	.10
Attributed neutralization			.15	.16	.14	.13	.08	.03	.14	.01	.08	.02
Anomia					.71	.69	.05	.12	.15	.11	.03	.11
Juvenile anomia							.03	.11	.18	.10	.07	.12
Family anomia									.21	.31	.23	.33
School anomia											.16	.25

assumed that these friends are likely to be other local youth of about the same age, then the data also tend to support the hypothesis that attributions of neutralization will significantly overestimate the actual level of personal neutralization which exists among the friends of the respondents. As to whether attributed neutralization will be related to basic norm violation among rurban sixth graders at a higher level of confidence than will personal neutralization, the data in Table 3 shows support for this hypothesis with the boys only. Neither personal neutralization nor attributed neutralization was significantly related to basic norm violation among the girls. As Table 5 indicates, the other independent variables have little effect when controlled. The statistically significant zero-order correlation obtained for the boys declines only slightly, maintaining significance in every instance.

The mean Srole Scale scores shown in Table 2 were not significantly different for the boys and the girls, nor was either significantly different from that obtained for the previously mentioned sample of 125 15-18-year-old boys from the high delinquency urban area. Both means were, however, significantly lower (P < .001) than the mean score obtained for the sample of 115 institutionalized delinquent boys. As is indicated in Table 3, no significant relationship was found between scores on the Srole Scale and basic norm violation among the boys. Table 3 does, however, show a modest but statistically significant relationship between scores on the Srole Scale and basic norm violation among the girls. The theoretical relationship between these variables, the fact that the correlation was rather low, and the pattern of statistically significant intercorrelations among the various meausres of anomia led us to control for the effect of juvenile anomia, family anomia, and school anomia. We find that all these juvenile anomia variables account for the relationship between basic norm violation and Srole Scale scores. As is indicated in Table 5, this relationship declines to statistical insignificance (τ xy.z = .01, P > .05) when juvenile anomia is controlled, and to statistical insignificance (τ xy.z = .06, P > .05) when either family anomia or school anomia is controlled. Self-concept is the only other variable

Table 5: PARTIAL CORRELATION COEFFICIENTS FOR BASIC NORM VIOLATION AND VARIOUS INDEPENDENT VARIABLES WITH CONTROL VARIABLES HELD CONSTANT FOR 398 MALE AND 451 FEMALE RURBAN, WHITE, WORKING-CLASS SIXTH GRADERS

Original Independent Variable	Personal Neutralization		Attributed Neutralization		Anomia		Juvenile Anomia		Family Anomia		School Anomia		Self-Concept	
	Boys	Girls	Boys	Girls	Boys	Girls	Boys	Girls	Boys	Girls	Boys	Girls	Boys	Girls
Personal neutralization	—	—	.02	*	.08	*	.08	*	.07	*	.08	*	.04	*
Attributed neutralization	.13	*	—	—	.15	*	.14	*	.14	*	.14	*	.14	*
Anomia	*	.08	*	.08	—	—	*	.01	*	.06	*	.06	*	.05
Juvenile anomia	.08	.11	.07	.11	.08	.07	—	—	.08	.11	.07	.11	.07	.09
Family anomia	.12	.15	.12	.15	.13	.12	.13	.12	—	—	.11	.09	.07	.04
School anomia	.07	.16	.06	.16	.08	.16	.07	.15	.06	.13	—	—	.04	.10
Self-concept	.27	.28	.27	.28	.28	.27	.28	.27	.26	.25	.27	.25	—	—

*Zero-order correlation not statistically significant. No partial correlation computation necessary.

[112]

which can also account for the relationship; the correlation declines to statistical insignificance (τ xy.z = .05, P > .05) when self-concept is controlled.

The mean juvenile anomia scores shown in Table 2 were not significantly different for the boys and the girls. As is shown in Table 3, there was a significant positive relationship between juvenile anomia and basic norm violation. Despite the inter-correlations, the data in Table 5 show that none of the other independent variables, including the Srole Scale itself, can account for this relationship. The fact that Juvenile Anomia Index scores can account for the positive relationship discovered between Srole Scale scores and basic norm violation, but that Srole Scale scores cannot account for the relationship between Juvenile Anomia Index and basic norm violation, demonstrates the potential power of the age specific measure as a possible predictor of such norm violation.

There was no significant difference between the mean family anomia scores shown for boys and girls in Table 2. As Table 3 shows, these scores are significantly related to basic norm violation for both sexes. When we control for the effect of self-concept, the correlations decline appreciably, holding statistical significance for the boys, but falling to statistical insignificance for the girls. Despite the pronounced intercorrelations, none of the other independent variables showed appreciable effect upon the zero-order correlations.

The mean school anomia scores shown in Table 2 are not significantly different for the boys and the girls. Table 3 indicates a significant positive relationship between school anomia scores and basic norm violation, with the zero-order correlation somewhat more pronounced for the girls. When self-concept is controlled, the relationship remains statistically significant among the girls but falls to statistical insignificance (τ xy.z = .04, P > .05) for the boys. With control of family anomia or attributed neutralization, the relationship between school anomia and basic norm violation remains statistically significant among the girls, but drops to statistical insignificance (τ xy.z = .06, P > .05) for the boys.

The mean self-concept scores shown in Table 2 are significantly different for the boys and the girls, with the mean for the boys significantly higher (P < .05) or less "favorable" than that for the girls. As is shown in Table 3, the hypothesis of a significant relationship between unfavorable self-concept scores and basic norm violation among rurban sixth graders was supported for both boys and girls, and the relationship appears to be somewhat similar. As Table 5 shows, none of the other independent variables has more than a negligible effect upon these zero-order correlations.

CONCLUSIONS

The pattern of basic norm violations which we have obtained is not surprising. The extent to which boys exceed girls even at this age is worth more consideration. In this connection, it is particularly unfortunate that the Nye-Short item dealing with sexual behavior could not have been used; one might expect boys to be more involved in drinking, driving, and property destruction, but the issue of sexual behavior is much less clear from past delinquency research. For those concerned with the attitudes of youth, the fact that levels of norm neutralization and anomia are high or higher among these youth than among older youth in a high delinquency area, and that the scores of the girls are essentially the same as those of the boys, suggests the need for careful research to determine the source of such attitudes.

Our initial research relating norm neutralization to male delinquency (Ball, 1966) showed neutralization to be significant in explaining the *emergence* of delinquency to the point of juvenile court appearances but found no consistently significant relationship which might explain either the *persistence* of delinquent behavior or the *severity* of offenses. Now it appears that *attributed* neutralization is actually the important form of neutralization among *males* and that a significant positive relationship between personal neutralization and basic norm violation occurs *only if self-concept scores are "unfavorable."* Neither form of neutralization appears to have much relevance to emergent delinquency among *females,* but it is apparent that this is not simply the result of the greater prevalence of social fictions among boys, for the girls attribute just as much norm neutralization to their friends as do the boys. The data instead suggest that the boys are more likely to *act* on the basis of the mistaken attributions than are the girls. This may mean that the violations we have examined happen to be male offenses, and that a set of norm violations more commonly associated with females would disclose a relationship. On the other hand, it is also possible that our measure of neutralization contains a sex bias and that a different measure employing different excuses might disclose the same relationship among the girls which we have found for the boys. It is also possible, of course, that the offenses of the boys are such that neutralization will be a significant factor while the offenses of the girls may not involve this set of attitudes at all. Aside from these and other possibilities, it remains to be seen whether our basic findings themselves will hold up with different age groups in different ecological settings.

Although the data with respect to anomia might be dismissed as the mere "acquiescence" of working-class respondents (Carr, 1971), the data also reflect appreciable levels of norm neutralization. It is difficult to discount this further evidence by any suggestion that a tendency to "acquiescence" would lead sixth graders to report acceptance of a variety of excuses for law violation which they did not really accept. Although the validity of the Srole Scale is somewhat questionable with adolescents, particularly because of "ambiguous items" which express "cliches" in "unilateral positive wording" (Carr, 1971:288), the fact is that corroborative data were obtained through use of the Family Anomia Index and the School Anomia Index, both of which include an equal number of positively and negatively worded items with very specific referents. The data do demonstrate the importance of anomia at this age and suggest the need for further development of measures of general anomia applicable to adolescents. The data also demonstrate the advantages to be gained by reconceptualizing anomia in terms of specific forms. The particular importance of family anomia among boys and school anomia among girls is somewhat unexpected given the literature which stresses the special significance of family life for girls and of the pressures of school on boys (Stern, 1964; Polk and Schafer, 1972).

Since the levels of norm neutralization and anomia among these youth are comparable to the levels to be found among older youth from high delinquency urban areas, or institutionalized delinquents, it seems clear that some factor is operating to minimize the likelihood that such attitudes will be expressed in delinquent behavior. While differential opportunity may be an important ecological factor, the data clearly show that we can generalize beyond the studies of Reckless and Dinitz and their associates. Self-concept may now be considered not only a factor which "insulates" boys against the pressures of a high delinquency urban area, but also as a factor which affects the risk of emergent delinquency in the form of basic norm violation among both boys and girls in a rurban area of relatively low delinquency risk. Self-concept appears to be a more significant factor in basic norm violation than is either neutralization or anomia, to the extent that it accounts for the apparent significance of personal neutralization among the rurban boys and certain forms of anomia, including school anomia among boys and family anomia among girls. Although it appears that the self-concept variable can be cautiously extended to studies of norm violation among females, it is also true that self-concept was the only independent variable which shared significantly different mean scores for the boys and the girls. If we recall that the Self-Concept Inventory really seems to be measuring *attribution* rather than internalization, it seems clear that the boys are more likely to believe that others expect them to be involved in trouble. Although it might be argued that sixth graders have not yet entered the years of highest delinquency risk and that self-concept might decline in significance under increased pressure, the evidence from high delinquency areas, where the pressure toward delinquency *is* great, leads us to expect that this variable will retain its significance with advancing age, perhaps becoming even more important (Reckless, 1967:475).

The need for more rigorous comparisons by age, sex, and ecological context is obvious. Although the present data do not allow racial comparison, this factor should certainly be examined. Gould (1969) has argued that the label of troublemaker is so commonly applied to blacks as to have little personal relevance to self-concept, and Jensen (1970:89) has produced some evidence in support of this contention. It may well be that self-concept bears a different relationship to various forms of delinquency among blacks than among whites.

Many problems remain to be faced, some of which have to do with the present focus upon basic norm violation and emergent delinquency. The narrow range of norm violation at this stage leaves open the possibility that greater variance will disclose different relationships than those described. Our research is organized in such a way as to permit us to deal empirically with certain aspects of this question at a later date, for we expect to follow this cohort to at least the ninth grade, where the range of delinquency should be broader. Although computations for their own sake have been deliberately avoided here, the increased likelihood of unjustified conclusions regarding statistical significance which results from the many comparisons which were necessary must also be dealt with in subsequent research. Finally, there is the possibility that the extent of relationship among sets of variables may be influenced by factors such as the validity of the measures employed and the variance of different dimensions tapped, so that one relationship may only *appear* to be more "pronounced" than another. All of these problems await further exploration.

NOTES

1. The census categories of "metropolitan central city," "metropolitan outside central city," and "nonmetropolitan" corresponded neither to the Uniform Crime Report categories of "city," "suburban," and "rural" nor to the categories of "urban," "semiurban," and "rural" used by DHEW for reporting delinquency.

2. Although the Nye-Short Scale was developed more than 20 years ago (Nye and Short, 1956) and has been criticized as a measure of "nuisance behavior" rather than serious delinquency (Clark and Wenninger, 1962), it remains particularly appropriate if regarded as a measure of basic norm violation. Unfortunately, school officials

insisted that one item, that dealing with sexual behavior, be deleted from the scale. This would have provided some very valuable data, especially for comparisons of male and female patterns. Nevertheless, the general approach is supported by the findings reported below, which show very little in the way of more "serious" offenses within the samples, but do disclose basic norm violations which can be treated as emergent delinquency.

3. Preliminary findings have been reported by Ball and Lilly (1971, 1976), but these earlier reports were kept very brief, with no attempt made to compare data by sex or to follow the data beyond zero-order correlations, mostly due to editorial constraints. Until now, it has not been possible to make the necessary comparisons or to clarify the notion of emergent delinquency which has been implicit in this research.

4. The Neutralization Inventory, described in detail elsewhere (Ball, 1966), is comprised of four situational subscales of 10 items each. For purposes of the present research, norm neutralization was measured by a more efficient Abridged Neutralization Inventory consisting of a subscale related to shoplifting, which has in previous research shown alpha coefficients of approximately .90 and correlations of .79 to .89 with scores for the entire inventory. The Attributed Neutralization Inventory is identical except that respondents are instructed to answer as they feel their friends would respond.

5. The Juvenile Anomia Index included four of the original Srole Scale items, the sole variation being that one item ("The older my friends and I get, the more disgusted we get with things") was substituted for an original ("Its hardly fair for adults to bring children into the world the way things look for the future"). Previous work (Ball, 1969) has traced a major part of the measurement error involved in the use of the Srole Scale with adolescents to the single item which was replaced.

6. The Family Anomia Index and the School Anomia Index consist of 10 items each, with the same five Likert-type response categories used on the Srole Scale according to a method of Edwards and Kirkpatrick (1948). The items parallel those of the Srole Scale except for specific references to parents and teachers. The Coefficients of Reproducibility for both indexes have exceeded .80. Beaver (1972) provides an extensive analysis of the items.

7. Since the previous research dealing with norm neutralization, anomia, and self-concept factors has reported central tendencies in terms of mean scores, using the t-test to establish the significance of differences, it is important to follow suit so as to facilitate comparisons. Although most of the argument over the use of parametric or nonparametric statistics has centered around the issue of measurement level, the basic norm violation scores pose an additional problem in that the scores do not approximate a normal distribution even with a large sample size. Because the various measures can be considered as essentially ordinal, Kendall's tau (τ) was used to test for relationships between the independent and dependent variables. For the sake of consistency, the significance of all t-tests was verified by a comparison of median scores. Although significance levels varied slightly, the findings showed no basic differences. This mixture of parametric and nonparametric statistical tests is somewhat unconventional, but it does appear to provide the nearest approximation to a solution.

8. Since there are limits to the liberties which may be taken with nonparametric statistics, and since the author feels that data manipulation ought to be governed by theoretical guidelines rather than empirical expedience, the various possibilities are examined one at a time, and more elaborate techniques are avoided here.

REFERENCES

BALL, R.A. (1966). "An empirical exploration of neutralization theory." Criminologica, 4(2):22-32.

——— (1969). "A comparison of incipient alienation, anomia and MMPI scores as indicators of delinquency." Criminologica, 6(4):13-24.

BALL, R.A., and LILLY, J.R. (1971). "Anomia and the sixth graders of Marion County." Criminology, 9(1):69-85.

——— (1976). "Female delinquency in a rurban county." Criminology, 14(2):279-281.

BEAVER, W. (1972). "Anomia and the sixth graders of Marion County." Unpublished M.A. thesis, West Virginia University.

CARR, L.C. (1971). "The Srole items and acquiescence." American Sociological Review, 36(2):280-293.

CLARK, J.P., and WENNINGER, E.P. (1962). "Socioeconomic class and areas as correlates of illegal behavior among juveniles." American Sociological Review, 27(6):826-834.

CLINARD, M. (1964). Anomie and deviant behavior. New York: Free Press.

DINITZ, S., RECKLESS, W.C., and KAY, B. (1958). "A self gradient among potential delinquents." Journal of Criminal Law, Criminology and Police Science, 49(2):230-233.

DINITZ, S., SCARPITTI, F.R., and RECKLESS, W.C. (1962). "Delinquency vulnerability: A cross group and longitudinal analysis." American Sociological Review, 27(4):515-517.

EDWARDS, A.L., and KIRKPATRICK, F.P. (1948). "A technique for the construction of attitude scales." Journal of Applied Psychology, 16(1):125-128.

GIBBONS, D.C. (1972). "Crime in the hinterland." Criminology, 10(2):177-192.

GOULD, L.C. (1969). "Who defines delinquency: A comparison of self-reported and officially reported indices of delinquency for three racial groups." Social Problems, 18(1):152-163.

HIRSCHI, T., and SELVIN, H.C. (1967). Delinquency research: An appraisal of analytic methods. New York: Free Press.

JARRETT, W.H., and HALER, A.O. (1964). "Situational and personal antecedents of incipient alienation: An exploratory study." Genetic Psychology Monographs, 69:151-191.

JENSEN, G.F. (1970). "Delinquency and adolescent self-conceptions: A study of the personal relevance of infraction." Social Problems, 20(1):84-103.

KAHL, J. (1957). The American class structure. New York: Holt, Rinehart and Winston.

LILLY, J.R. (1969). "Self factors and delinquency in a rural-urban county." Unpublished M.A. thesis, West Virginia University.

MARTIN, W. (1957). "Ecological change in satellite rural area." American Sociological Review, 22(2):173-183.

MATZA, D. (1964). Delinquency and drift. New York: John Wiley.

NYE, F.I., and SHORT, J. (1956). "Scaling delinquent behavior." American Sociological Review, 22(3):326-331.

ORCUTT, J.D. (1970). "Self concept and insulation against delinquency: Some critical notes." Sociological Quarterly, 11(4):381-391.

POLK, K. (1967). "Delinquency and community action in nonmetropolitan areas."

Pp. 343-352 in President's Commission on Law Enforcement and Criminal Justice, Task Force report: Juvenile delinquency and youth crime. Washington, D.C.: U.S. Government Printing Office.

POLK, K., and SCHAFER, W.E. (1972). Schools and delinquency. Englewood Cliffs, N.J.: Prentice-Hall.

RECKLESS, W.C. (1967). The crime problem. New York: Appleton-Century-Crofts.

RECKLESS, W.C., and DINITZ, S. (1967). "Pioneering with self-concept as a vulnerability factor in delinquency." Journal of Criminal Law, Criminology and Police Science, 58(4):515-523.

RECKLESS, W.C., DINITZ, S., and KAY, B. (1957). "The self component in potential delinquency and potential non-delinquency." American Sociological Review, 22(4):566-570.

RECKLESS, W.C., DINITZ, S., and MURRAY, E. (1956). "Self concept as insulator against delinquency." American Sociological Review, 21(5):744-764.

——— (1957). "The good boy in a high delinquency area." Journal of Criminal Law, Criminology and Police Science, 48(2):18-26.

RECKLESS, W.C., and SHOHAM, S. (1963). "Norm containment theory as applied to delinquency and crime." Excerpta Criminologica, 3(6):637-644.

SCARPITTI, F.R., MURRAY, E., DINITZ, S., and RECKLESS, W.C. (1960). "The good boys in a high delinquency area: Four years later." American Sociological Review, 25(6):922-926.

SCHWARTZ, M., and TANGRI, S. (1965). "A note on self-concept as an insulator against delinquency." American Sociological Review, 30(6):922-926.

SROLE, L. (1956). "Social integration and certain corallaries: An exploratory study." American Sociological Review, 21(5):709-716.

STEPHEN, C. (1973). "Attribution of intention and perception of attitude as functions of liking and similarity." Sociometry, 36(4):463-475.

STERN, R.S. (1964). Delinquent conduct and broken homes. New Haven, Conn.: College and University Press.

STINCHCOMBE, A. (1964). Rebellion in a high school. Chicago: Quadrangle Books.

SYKES, G., and MATZA, D. (1957). "Techniques of neutralization: A theory of delinquency." American Sociological Review, 22(6):664-673.

TANGRI, S., and SCHWARTZ, M. (1967). "Delinquency research and the self-concept variable." Journal of Criminal Law, Criminology and Police Science, 58(2):182-190.

TRIANDIS, H.C., and DAVIS, E.E. (1965). "Race and belief as determinants of behavioral intentions." Journal of Personality and Social Psychology, 2(5):715-725.

Roy L. Austin
*The Pennsylvania
State University*

7

COMMITMENT,
NEUTRALIZATION, AND
DELINQUENCY

The works of Cohen (1955), Miller (1958), and Cloward and
Ohlin (1960) are sufficiently influential to be potential classics
in the study of delinquent subcultures; but contrary to the
position evident in these works, Matza claims that "the
subculture of delinquency . . . does not commit adherents to
their misdeeds" (1964:50). As in his earlier publications with
Sykes (1957, 1961), he proposed that delinquents are attached
to conventional values but periodically neutralize these values
to commit illegal offenses. His arguments on neutralization and
commitment are persuasive and have received apparent empirical support (Matza, 1964; Ball, 1968; Buffalo and Rodgers,
1971). This study will reexamine Matza's position on the
relationship of commitment and neutralization to delinquency.
The empirical evidence supposedly favoring Matza will be
evaluated and a new empirical analysis will be conducted.

COMMITMENT AND DELINQUENCY

One of the most important questions raised by Matza
concerns the proportion of delinquents who are unconvention-

AUTHOR'S NOTE: I appreciate the helpful comments of Theodore Ferdinand on an
earlier draft of this manuscript.

ally committed. He claims that delinquency occurs only intermittently and that the majority of delinquents (60% to 85%) do not become adult criminals. Since his definition of commitment[1] precludes availability of unconventionally committed delinquents for nondelinquent activities and for maturational reform, he argues that most delinquents are *not* unconventionally committed. However, Matza's definition of commitment is based on a misinterpretation of Kornhauser's (1962:321-322) use of this concept because Kornhauser's committed radicals and liberals participated in activities unrelated to their political work. Also, Kornhauser discussed conditions under which these persons lost their commitment.

Another logical problem in Matza is the judgment that unconventional commitment is not important in the study of delinquency since only the 15% to 40% of delinquents who become adult criminals are so committed. However, these are the delinquents regarded as most harmful to a community; and a variable (commitment) which differentiates between serious delinquents and other delinquents must be more important than Matza allows.

Matza's empirical evidence for a relatively small proportion of unconventionally committed delinquents is also problematic. He claims that his results show that *2%* of institutionalized delinquent boys approved of the companionship of boys shown committing delinquent offenses in pictures; 40% were indifferent, 30% disapproved mildly, and 28% expressed indignation (1964:49). Matza (1964:50) interprets the virtual absence of positive approval of the perpetrator of delinquent acts as favorable to his position; but his categorization of responses like "I could hang out with him or not" and "it would make me no difference" as indifference (1964:50) is questionable. These responses, especially for institutionalized boys, may be interpreted as "it wouldn't bother me" which is neither indifference nor neutrality but a form of tolerance.

Should my interpretation of Matza's "indifference" responses be correct, then a majority of the delinquents were, at least, tolerant of persons guilty of stealing a bike, vandalism, stealing from a car, or stealing from a warehouse (64%, 59%, 52%, and

51%, respectively). It is instructive, also, that in this institutionalized and therefore relatively serious delinquent population Matza's allowance for 15% to 40% unconventionally committed grossly overestimates the 2% yielded by his interpretation. In any case, the ambiguous indifference category cannot bear the burden of supporting his argument against commitment.

The results of Buffalo and Rodgers (1971) that supposedly support Matza's position on commitment are no less equivocal than Matza's results. Buffalo and Rodgers show that when institutionalized delinquents are asked what they *should* do in given situations, as many as 88.6% exhibit familiarity with conventional expectations. They interpret this finding as evidence that the moral norms of delinquents "are not in contradiction to those of the dominant society" (1971:103); but their results also show that as many as 55.3% of the delinquents chose the most deviant solution when asked what they *would* do in given situations. Further, no more than 37.2% ever selected the solution closest to social expectations in response to this question. There is likely to be disagreement over which question (the should or would) is the better indicator of the moral norms accepted by the delinquents.

Empirical evidence that rejects Matza's argument against commitment of delinquents to their misdeeds has also been reported. Hindelang (1970) has shown that in a sample of noninstitutionalized boys 82% of the drinkers, 66% of the fighters, and 63% of the sexually promiscuous approved of their delinquent acts. However, there is some agreement that the middle-class sample and the relatively innocuous acts used by Hindelang limit the value of the study as a test of Matza's thesis (Spector, 1971; Hindelang, 1971).

The disagreement between the researchers and the contradictory conclusions suggested by the reported research recommend another examination of empirical evidence on the question of the proportion of delinquents who are unconventionally committed. The hypothesis to be tested is stated to agree with Matza.

Hypothesis 1. No more than 40% of delinquents hold unconventional beliefs.

NEUTRALIZATION AND DELINQUENCY

Matza (1964:61-62) argues that the criminal law states conditions under which the law is inapplicable; and delinquents likewise claim inapplicability of the law by denying responsibility for their acts, denying injury or victimization, or utilizing other similar "techniques of neutralization." These techniques allow delinquents to violate norms while retaining allegiance to them; and criminal law is especially susceptible to neutralization.

Ball (1968) reports empirical support for Matza's neutralization "theory" in his finding that delinquents score higher than nondelinquents on a neutralization inventory. His findings indeed suggest that youths who employ neutralizing techniques are more likely to be delinquent than youths who do not employ such techniques; that is, neutralization may be a cause of delinquency as Matza contends. However, Ball's results also suggest a logical flaw in Matza's arguments or a problem in operationalizing neutralization. If, as Matza claims, serious delinquents are the only unconventionally committed delinquents, then *serious delinquents should not hold beliefs requiring neutralization.*

Ball's results show that serious delinquents (institutionalized delinquents) are more likely to employ neutralization than nondelinquents. Therefore, assuming that serious delinquents are more unconventional in beliefs than nondelinquents, Matza's proposed function for the neutralizing techniques may be erroneous. So-called neutralizing techniques may not remove moral obstacles and thereby allow delinquency. Alternatively, the indicators of neutralization may be indicators of unconventional beliefs and Ball's results are consistent with the expectation, even by Matza, that such beliefs are more likely among serious delinquents. Thus, the operationalization of neutralization by Sykes and Matza must be examined.

Distinguishing between beliefs that serve to neutralize conventional bonds and beliefs that show unconventional commitment is a major operational problem in neutralization theory. Matza implies that neutralizing beliefs (denial of injury, etc.) are not constraining, and persons holding such beliefs are therefore not committed to any course of action; but constraint lies in the strength with which a belief is held rather than in the nature of the belief. For instance, whether the neutralizing belief that drunks deserve to be rolled is constrained with respect to behavior toward drunks depends on the intensity with which the belief is held. Likewise, the constraining effect of the belief that middle-class norms are unworthy of respect (Cohen, 1955) is determined by intensity. Further, differential effects of the two beliefs on behavior do not necessarily indicate differences in commitment. Each belief should encourage behaviors consistent with the sphere of action (rolling drunks or wanton destruction of property) relevant to the belief. Thus, Matza's substitution of neutralization for commitment is questionable. Indeed, following the logic of the absence of constraint in neutralizing beliefs leaves us with a phenomenon that may be nonexistent and therefore incapable of operationalization.

Another operational problem in neutralization theory is revealed when one inquires into the construct reflected by indicators of neutralization. Neutralization indicators, as well as indicators of commitment to misdeeds, seem to reflect unconventionality. For instance, one basis of neutralization mentioned by Matza is the delinquent's extension of the concept of self-defense beyond the legal conception; and Matza implies that the delinquent may *strongly* believe in his conception and not be unconventionally committed. However, the extralegal status of the delinquent's concept of self-defense is likely to make the conception unconventional; and it is awareness of the conception and the cost the delinquent is willing to bear (an indication of the strength with which it is held) for maintaining it that determines his commitment to it (Becker, 1960). That is, neutralization can imply unconventional commitment. Therefore, it may be more useful to differentiate between degrees of commitment to unconventional beliefs rather than opposing neutralization to unconventional commitment. Of course, the sphere of reference of the belief will also be relevant in explaining behavior.

Three hypotheses will guide empirical investigation of the operational problems in neutralization theory. Hypothesis 2 deals with the relationship between neutralizing beliefs and unconventional beliefs. If neutralizing beliefs occur more frequently among otherwise conventional youths than among the unconventional, Matza would appear to be correct. If the finding is reversed, there is the suggestion that indicators of neutralization reflect unconventionality. Hypotheses 3 and 4 will guide the search for more evidence favorable to the latter interpretation and will allow a test of the proposition that an actor can be committed to a neutralizing belief. The hypotheses are stated to support Matza.

Hypothesis 2. Youths who are conventionally committed are more likely to employ neutralization than youths who are unconventionally committed.

Hypothesis 3. Indicators of neutralization are more strongly related to one another than to indicators of unconventional commitment. (An opposite result suggests that a relatively large part of the variance in neutralization is explained by unconventionality.)

Hypothesis 4. An increase in the strength of unconventional beliefs makes delinquency more likely; but an increase in the strength of neutralization beliefs will not result in an increase in delinquency. (Rejection of the second part suggests increasing constraint on behavior as the strength of the neutralizing belief increases and is contrary to Matza's suggestion that neutralizing beliefs cannot commit.)

RELATIVE IMPORTANCE OF
NEUTRALIZATION AND COMMITMENT

Neutralization theory was proposed as an alternative to delinquent subculture theories in which unconventional commitment plays a "key role" (Matza, 1964:19). Therefore, it is important to determine whether commitment or neutralization is more important in understanding delinquency. Hypotheses 5 and 6 will provide an answer to this question and again are stated to support Matza.

Hypothesis 5. The relationship between neutralization and delinquency is stronger than the relationship between commitment and delinquency.

Hypothesis 6. When other variables are controlled, variation in neutralization results in more change in delinquency than variation in commitment.

THE SAMPLE AND DATA COLLECTION[2]

A stratified probability sample of 5,545 students was elected from youths expected to enter junior and senior high schools in western Contra Costa County, California, during fall 1964. Of these students, 4,077 blacks, Caucasians, and Orientals of both sexes completed questionnaires for the Richmond Youth Project in spring 1965. Only the 1,588 Caucasian boys are used in this study.

MEASUREMENT OF VARIABLES

Many discussions of commitment (Becker, 1960; Gerard, 1968) suggest that an adequate constitutive definition of this concept will include the elements of cost and awareness; that is, a person is not committed to a course of action unless he is aware of some cost attending contrary behavior. However, Matza never explicitly claims that cost and awareness are elements in the commitment he sees in subcultural theories; and Cohen (1955:30) clearly states that members of delinquent gangs pay little attention to "remoter gains and costs." Therefore, in measuring commitment our concern is with finding beliefs "with a definite if unconventional moral flavor" (Cohen, 1955:35). It is this characterization of subcultural beliefs that Matza questions in proposing subterranean traditions that emphasize similarities between conventional culture and the subculture of delinquency.

The variables in this study are operationalized as follows:

A. *Commitment*

1. Illegality: It is alright to get around the law if you can get away with it. (1) Strongly agree . . . (5) Strongly disagree.

2. Immorality: To get ahead you have to do some things that are not right. (1) Strongly agree . . . (5) Strongly disagree.

B. *Neutralization*

3. Not Hurt: Most things that people call delinquency really don't hurt anyone. (1) Strongly agree . . . (5) Strongly disagree.

4. Suckers: Suckers deserve to be taken advantage of. (1) Strongly agree . . . (5) Strongly disagree.

C. *Delinquency*

5. Minor Theft: Have you ever taken little things (worth less than $2.00) that did not belong to you? (1) No, never, (2) More than a year ago, (3) During the last year, (4) During the last year and more than a year ago.

6. Moderate Theft: Have you ever taken things of some value (between $2.00 and $50.00) that did not belong to you? Responses as for item 5.

7. Major Theft: Have you ever taken things of large value (worth over $50.00) that did not belong to you? Responses as for item 5.

8. Auto Theft: Have you ever taken a car for a ride without the owner's permission? Responses as for item 5.

9. Vandalism: Have you ever banged up something that did not belong to you on purpose? Responses as for item 5.

10. Assault: Not counting fights you may have had with a brother or sister, have you ever beaten up on anyone or hurt anyone on purpose? Responses as for item 5.

FINDINGS

1. Unconventional Commitment. In Table 1, 42% of the boys admitting major theft show unconventional commitment as judged by agreement with the immorality item. Also, between 43% and 57% of the boys admitting thefts other than minor ones show unconventional commitment as measured by a combination of the immorality and illegality items. Therefore, Matza's 15% to 40% of unconventionally committed delin-

Table 1: PERCENTAGE OF SELF-REPORTED DELINQUENTS EXPRESSING
WILLINGNESS TO VIOLATE THE LAW (ILLEGALITY) AND/OR
WILLINGNESS TO VIOLATE CONVENTIONAL NORMS (IMMORALITY)

Delinquency	Illegality	Immorality	Illegality and/or Immorality
Minor theft	14.8	24.5	30.8
Moderate theft	25.9	32.9	45.6
Major theft	36.1	42.9	57.1
Auto theft	26.7	33.1	43.1
Vandalism	19.9	30.4	37.4
Assault	16.2	24.1	30.5

quents is an underestimate. Further, the sample members who did not complete the questionnaire have a lower mean verbal score than other sample members (Wilson et al., n.d.) and are therefore likely to be more serious delinquents. Thus, the inclusion of data for missing sample members should increase the discrepancy in Matza's estimate, perhaps placing vandalism in the underestimate category. With the exception of assault then (and probably vandalism), Hypothesis 1 is rejected, more than 40% of delinquents showing unconventional commitment.

Table 1 also shows that the percentage of delinquents who may be adjudged as unconventionally committed is influenced by the measure of commitment used. Thus, for illegal beliefs, only one type of offense (major theft) shows more than 30% unconventionally committed. On the other hand, for immoral beliefs, four offenses show more than 30% so committed. That is, unconventional commitment is less likely in the normative area given greater importance by society through the passage of laws than in the extralegal normative area. This finding contradicts Matza's claim that the criminal law is especially susceptible to neutralization. Instead, delinquents are more likely to be committed to deviant beliefs that are not contrary to any law. In addition, the findings suggest the need for care in drawing conclusions from single indicators.

The results for the combined items in Table 1 are also consistent with the interpretation we earlier gave to Matza's (1964:49) empirical findings. Accepting the meaning we give to his indifference column, stealing and vandalism in his data reject Hypothesis 1, 51% to 64% of the delinquents being apparently unconventionally committed. On the other hand, Matza's findings for assault (mugging, fighting with a weapon, and armed robbery) show, respectively, 14%, 21%, and 24% unconventionally committed and support the hypothesis, as does our finding for assault. Even the larger proportion unconventionally committed among the thieves in Matza's data than in ours may be explained. His institutionalized sample should contain more serious delinquents than our sample of junior high and high school students.

2. *Construct Validity of Neutralization Indicators.* Table 2 shows a strong positive relationship between commitment and neutralization while Hypothesis 2 predicts a negative relationship. Clearly, the most unconventional boys (strongly agree) are the ones most likely to hold neutralizing beliefs. This finding is inconsistent with the proposition that neutralizing beliefs remove moral restraint because unconventional boys are less likely than conventional boys to have any moral restraint to be removed. However, the finding is consistent with an interpretation of neutralizing beliefs as unconventional beliefs; and further support for this interpretation is provided by Table 3.

In Table 3, willingness to use illegal behavior should reflect greater unconventionality than willingness to use immoral behavior which includes violation of extralegal norms. Contrary to Hypothesis 3, the indicator of the former (illegality) has the strongest relationship to the two neutralization indicators, this

Table 2: RELATIONSHIP BETWEEN COMMITMENT (ILLEGALITY) AND NEUTRALIZATION (NOT HURT)

	Commitment				
Neutralization	Strongly Agree	Agree	Undecided	Disagree	Strongly Disagree
Strongly agree	32.8	14.3	6.8	2.8	5.2
Agree	18.0	28.6	23.2	19.3	11.4
Undecided	23.0	31.9	41.1	36.9	27.7
Disagree	16.4	19.3	23.2	35.0	30.1
Strongly disagree	9.8	5.9	5.7	6.0	25.5
Number of cases	(16)	(119)	(263)	(580)	(498)

Tau B = .236
Significance = 0.0

Table 3: ZERO-ORDER CORRELATION COEFFICIENT MATRIX FOR
COMMITMENT INDICATORS (ILLEGALITY, IMMORALITY)
AND NEUTRALIZATION INDICATORS (SUCKERS, NOT HURT)

	Illegality	Immorality	Suckers
Not hurt	.226	.135	.167
Illegality		.257	.256
Immorality			.244

relationship being substantially greater than that between neutralization indicators. That is, the neutralization indicators have more in common with an indicator of serious unconventionality than with each other. Therefore, they may also be regarded as indicators of unconventionality.

The final step in examining the construct validity of neutralization is to determine whether neutralizing beliefs can constrain the believer to a course of action. The results shown in Table 4 partially agree with the commitment portion of Hypothesis 4 and reject the neutralization portion. All of the relationships are significant (Table 5) and show that delinquency is more likely among boys admitting commitment or neutralization. But it is the agree and strongly agree categories that allow a test of Hypothesis 4, which predicts a positive relationship between the strength of unconventional beliefs and delinquency involvement, while no such relationship is expected for neutralizing beliefs. These categories show that for willingness to violate the law (illegality), one of the commitment items, delinquency increases with the strength of the belief only for the two most serious acts, major theft and auto theft (one indicator of seriousness of offense is the proportion denying involvement). It appears that this belief is sufficiently unconventional that any degree of agreement is sufficient to maximize the likelihood of delinquency for all but serious thefts (one indicator of the degree of unconventionality reflected by the belief items is the proportion of boys who agree with the belief). Willingness to engage in immoral acts (immorality), the other commitment item, shows a similar pattern except that the next most serious offense, moderate theft, also satisfies the predicted pattern. For the neutralization beliefs, increase in strength is accompanied by an increase in the likelihood of

Table 4: PERCENTAGE OF WHITE BOYS DENYING INVOLVEMENT IN NAMED
DELINQUENT OFFENSES WITHIN CATEGORIES OF COMMITMENT
AND NEUTRALIZATION (Number of cases in parentheses)

	Strongly Agree	Agree	Undecided	Disagree	Strongly Disagree
A. Minor Theft					
Not hurt	37.2 (94)	37.3 (271)	48.2 (506)	47.2 (443)	60.2 (186)
Suckers	32.2 (87)	40.0 (185)	46.6 (309)	49.8 (582)	51.4 (216)
Illegality	32.8 (61)	32.5 (114)	34.2 (257)	45.9 (575)	59.8 (495)
Immorality	37.5 (64)	35.7 (213)	38.1 (252)	50.4 (552)	60.3 (290)
B. Moderate Theft					
Not hurt	68.1 (94)	74.2 (275)	79.8 (509)	86.2 (443)	88.8 (187)
Suckers	69.0 (87)	74.7 (186)	79.4 (311)	85.2 (587)	84.7 (216)
Illegality	60.7 (61)	56.1 (114)	74.0 (258)	81.6 (580)	92.4 (497)
Immorality	63.5 (63)	72.4 (214)	74.8 (254)	86.6 (553)	90.1 (293)
C. Major Theft					
Not hurt	83.0 (94)	92.0 (276)	94.7 (508)	95.3 (444)	95.2 (188)
Suckers	87.5 (88)	90.0 (186)	93.6 (311)	96.3 (587)	94.9 (216)
Illegality	74.2 (62)	83.3 (114)	92.7 (259)	94.5 (580)	97.8 (497)
Immorality	77.8 (63)	89.7 (214)	93.7 (255)	96.0 (555)	96.6 (293)
D. Auto Theft					
Not hurt	78.9 (95)	83.6 (274)	90.4 (513)	91.5 (446)	95.3 (190)
Suckers	79.8 (89)	86.6 (187)	91.4 (314)	92.0 (589)	93.5 (216)
Illegality	74.2 (62)	76.7 (116)	85.4 (260)	90.0 (581)	95.6 (501)
Immorality	79.7 (64)	85.5 (214)	85.3 (258)	92.8 (558)	96.3 (295)
E. Vandalism					
Not hurt	64.6 (96)	66.7 (276)	75.0 (509)	79.3 (439)	78.3 (189)
Suckers	59.1 (88)	68.4 (187)	71.2 (309)	80.2 (585)	81.6 (217)
Illegality	54.1 (61)	59.0 (117)	65.3 (259)	76.4 (576)	83.9 (498)
Immorality	60.9 (64)	61.3 (212)	69.9 (256)	79.1 (556)	82.2 (292)
F. Assault					
Not hurt	41.1 (95)	46.7 (276)	57.6 (512)	64.9 (444)	68.9 (190)
Suckers	40.2 (87)	52.4 (187)	55.0 (311)	62.3 (591)	67.6 (216)
Illegality	45.2 (62)	40.9 (115)	47.5 (259)	56.4 (582)	72.1 (498)
Immorality	56.3 (64)	49.3 (215)	49.2 (254)	63.4 (557)	66.8 (295)

All relationships are significant (tau B) at a probability of less than .001.

delinquency (except for not hurt with minor theft); that is, there appears to be increasing constraint to a course of action, and therefore increasing commitment, as the strength of these beliefs increase.

The finding that increased commitment is possible for neutralization items questions Matza's use of this concept as an alternative to commitment. Increasing commitment to neutralizing beliefs has different effects on delinquency than increasing commitment to the other unconventional beliefs in this study;

Table 5: TAU B AND SIGNIFICANCE FOR THE RELATIONSHIP BETWEEN
DELINQUENCY AND NEUTRALIZATION AND DELINQUENCY
AND COMMITMENT

	Neutralization				Commitment			
	Not Hurt		Suckers		Illegality		Immorality	
Delinquency	Tau B	Sig	Tau B	Sig	Tau B	Sig	Tau B	Sig
Minor theft	−.099	.000	−.108	.000	−.216	.0	−.167	.000
Moderate theft	−.129	.000	−.105	.000	−.235	.0	−.173	.000
Major theft	−.077	.001	−.079	.001	−.166	.000	−.124	.000
Auto theft	−.117	.000	−.084	.000	−.171	.000	−.142	.000
Vandalism	−.095	.000	−.132	.000	−.190	.000	−.152	.000
Assault	−.158	.000	−.124	.000	−.185	.000	−.127	.000

In all cases, boys who admit neutralization or unconventionality are more likely to be
delinquents.

but this difference seems to result from differences in the
extent to which the beliefs deviate from conventional beliefs,
not from an inability of neutralizing beliefs to commit to
unconventionality. Matza's concept of subterranean tradition
embodies this idea of beliefs differing in their deviation from
conventionality. However, the range of deviation that qualifies a
belief for the subterranean label remains unstated. Moreover, a
dichotomy of unconventional beliefs with subterranean traditions as one category seems to have less scientific utility than a
conception involving degree of unconventionality and degree of
commitment, both of which encourage measurement above the
nominal level.

3. *Explanatory Import of Commitment and Neutralization.*
The results in Table 5 reject Hypothesis 5, there being only one
case out of 24 in which a relationship between delinquency and
neutralization is stronger than that between delinquency and
commitment. This exception occurs for assault and denial of
injury (not hurt) and exceeds only the relationship between
assault and willingness to behave immorally (immorality).
However, a somewhat more complex picture emerges when the
relationship between each independent variable and delinquency is examined with the other variables controlled (Table
6).

For the theft offenses (minor theft through auto theft) in
Table 6, the significance of the unstandardized regression

Table 6: RESULTS FOR THE STEPWISE REGRESSION OF DELINQUENCY ON COMMITMENT (ILLEGAL, IMMORAL) AND NEUTRALIZATION (NOT HURT, SUCKERS)

	B	Beta	Significance of B
Minor Theft			
Illegal	−.08	−.10	.001
Immoral	−.07	−.10	.001
Not hurt	−.05	−.08	.001
Suckers	−.02	−.03	N.S.
Moderate Theft			
Illegal	−.10	−.17	.001
Immoral	−.07	−.14	.001
Not hurt	−.04	−.09	.001
Suckers	−.01	−.02	N.S.
Major Theft			
Illegal	−.05	−.16	.001
Immoral	−.03	−.10	.001
Not hurt	−.01	−.04	N.S.
Suckers	−.00	−.01	N.S.
Auto Theft			
Illegal	−.03	−.06	.001
Immoral	−.04	−.12	.001
Not hurt	−.03	−.08	.001
Suckers	−.01	−.04	N.S.
Vandalism			
Illegal	−.04	−.07	.001
Immoral	−.07	−.13	.001
Not hurt	−.04	−.07	.001
Suckers	−.05	−.09	.001
Assault			
Illegal	−.08	−.10	.001
Immoral	−.05	−.09	.001
Not hurt	−.07	−.11	.001
Suckers	−.04	−.06	.001

B = Unstandardized regression coefficient
Beta = Standardized regression coefficient

coefficients show that suckers, one of the neutralization variables, makes no significant contribution to the prediction of delinquency. For major theft, neither neutralization variable makes a significant contribution. However, for vandalism and assault, the four independent variables make a significant contribution.

In Table 6 also, the beta coefficients show that, with the exception of assault, a commitment indicator always causes the greatest change in delinquency; and for theft, excepting auto theft, both commitment items are more important in influencing change in delinquency than either neutralization item, illegality being particularly influential. Therefore, of the six types of delinquency examined, only for assault is Hypothesis 6 supported, a neutralization indicator causing slightly more change in assault than either commitment indicator.

SUMMARY AND CONCLUSIONS

Matza (1964) underestimated the proportion of delinquents who are unconventionally committed and remained unaware of the underestimate because of an improper interpretation of his empirical results. Our findings, which show more unconventionality among delinquents than Matza allows, are consistent with a reinterpretation of his results. The similarity in results includes the indication that assaulters are less likely to be unconventionally committed than other kinds of delinquents. Such a finding is scarcely surprising given the cultural support for adolescent males to display masculinity.

The subdivision of beliefs by Matza into two opposed classes, neutralizing and committing, is misleading and should be replaced by an unconventionality continuum. This recommendation is supported especially by the finding that two of the traditional indicators of neutralization have more in common with willingness to break the law than with each other. The unconventionality continuum will allow recognition of the extent of similarity or difference between the beliefs supporting delinquency and conventional beliefs; but unlike Matza's classification and arguments, it should not support the inference that the less unconventional beliefs cannot commit a person to a course of action. Our findings suggest that *variation* in committing potential is greater for the less unconventional beliefs (neutralization) than for the more unconventional beliefs (commitment). One explanation of this differential variation is that those persons whose beliefs attain the outer limits of unconventionality have also attained the maximum likelihood of constraint to engage in less unconventional behaviors.

Therefore, for more unconventional beliefs the strength of the specific belief is positively related only to the most serious delinquent offenses like major theft.

Contrary to Matza's emphasis on neutralization and his criticism of commitment in subcultural theories, tabular analysis and stepwise regression show that more deviant beliefs have a stronger effect on delinquency than less deviant beliefs. In the terminology of the theorists involved, neutralizing beliefs or beliefs most likely to qualify as subterranean values have a weaker effect on delinquency than beliefs that are diametrically opposed to "middle-class values." Only for assault does a neutralizing belief assume equal importance with a more unconventional belief.

More generally, the importance given to beliefs in the older subcultural theories and in neutralization theory is supported by this study. While no systematic comparison was made with the explanatory import of other variables, the tau coefficients in Table 5 exceed those for class and for father-absence with delinquency using the same data, and the combined commitment items yield gamma coefficients of $-.34$, $-.51$, $-.62$, $-.50$, $-.42$, and $-.30$ with minor theft, moderate theft, major theft, auto theft, vandalism, and assault, respectively. These are higher coefficients than are usually reported for the relationship between other variables and delinquency.

It is safe to assume that, if brain damage is absent, persons exposed to the usual socializing influences in a human community will develop some moral restraint. Such restraint is neutralized with varying frequency through the acceptance of any unconventional belief, not only by the "neutralizing" beliefs. Further, the more unconventional the belief the more likely it is to result in serious violation of norms. Matza sometimes overlooks this positive relationship between unconventionality and norm violation in proposing an importance for marginal unconventionality that is rejected by the fact.

NOTES

1. According to Matza (1964:28), commitment implies "rendering oneself presently and in the future unavailable for other lines of action."
2. A more complete description may be found in Travis Hirschi (1969).

REFERENCES

BALL, R.A. (1968). "An empirical exploration of neutralization theory." Pp. 255-265 in M. Lefton, J. Skipper, and C. McCaghy (eds.), Approaches to deviance. New York: Appleton-Century-Crofts.

BECKER, H. (1960). "Notes on the concept of commitment." American Journal of Sociology, 66:32-40.

BUFFALO, M.D., and RODGERS, J.W. (1971). "Behavioral norms and attachment: Problems of deviance and conformity." Social Problems, 19(1):101-113.

CLOWARD, R., and OHLIN, L. (1960). Delinquency and opportunity: A theory of delinquent gangs. Glencoe, Ill.: Free Press.

COHEN, A. (1955). Delinquent boys. Glencoe, Ill.: Free Press.

——— (1965). "The sociology of the deviant act: Anomie theory and beyond." American Sociology Review, (February):5-14.

——— (1966). Deviance and control. Englewood Cliffs, N.J.: Prentice-Hall.

GERARD, H. (1968). "Basic features of commitment." Pp. 456-463 in R.P. Abelson et al. (eds), Theories of cognitive consistency: A sourcebook. Chicago: Rand McNally.

HINDELANG, M.J. (1970). "The commitment of delinquents to their misdeeds: Do delinquents drift?" Social Problems, 17(4):502-509.

——— (1971). "Reply to Spector." Social Problems, 18(3):422-424.

HIRSCHI, T. (1969). Causes of delinquency. Berkeley: University of California Press.

KORNHAUSER, W. (1962). "Social bases of commitment: A study of liberals and radicals." Pp. 321-339 in A. Rose (ed.), Human behavior and social processes. Boston: Houghton Mifflin.

MATZA, D. (1964). Delinquency and drift. New York: John Wiley.

MATZA, D., and SYKES, G. (1957). "Techniques of neutralization: A theory of delinquency." American Journal of Sociology, 22(December):664-670.

——— (1961). "Juvenile delinquency and subterranean values." Pp. 94-105 in R. Cavan (ed.), Readings in juvenile delinquency. New York: J.B. Lippincott.

MILLER, W. (1958). "Lower class culture as a generating milieu of gang delinquency." Journal of Social Issues, 14(3):5-19.

SPECTOR, M. (1971). "On 'do delinquents drift?' " Social Problems, 18(3):420-422.

WILSON, A., HIRSCHI, T., and ELDER, G. (n.d.). Richmond Youth Project; Secondary School Study. Technical report no. 1. Berkeley: Survey Research Center, University of California.

James T. Sprowls
Bruce Bullington
*The Pennsylvania
State University*

REMOVING JUVENILES
FROM CAMP HILL
A Case Study

In January of 1975, Dr. Jerome Miller, architect of the closing of juvenile institutions in Massachusetts, accepted a position in the Pennsylvania governor's office as Special Assistant for Community Programs. Shortly after his arrival Dr. Miller identified the juvenile population at the State Correctional Institution at Camp Hill as the target of what was intended as the first in a series of deinstitutionalization efforts. Although the Camp Hill facility was believed to contain the most dangerous and intractable youngsters in the state's delinquent population, there were several reasons for beginning with Camp Hill. First, the Pennsylvania Juvenile Act of 1972 (P.L. No. 1464) Section 27 requires that:

A child shall not be committed or transferred to a penal institution or other facility used primarily for the execution of sentences of adults convicted of a crime unless there is no appropriate facility available, in which case the child shall be kept separate at all times.

The Camp Hill facility, operated by the State Bureau of Corrections (all other juvenile institutions were either run by the Department of Public Welfare or were private) was the only state institution housing both adults and juveniles. Attempts to segregate the juvenile from the adult population had resulted in dramatic reductions in juvenile access to education, vocational training, and recreational opportunities. To the extent that the required separation was achieved, it was accomplished by keeping the juveniles within their cell blocks for periods up to, and in excess of, 20 hours per day. Miller reasoned that even his staunchest critics would have difficulty justifying the further detention of juveniles at Camp Hill under such conditions.

Second, if these youngsters, assumed to be the most dangerous and incorrigible members of the state's delinquent population, could be returned to the community without major disruptive consequences, the logic of maintaining lower risk youngsters in the less secure facilities operated by the Department of Public Welfare would be substantially undermined.

And finally, Miller believed that LEAA was interested in funding a community-based program for "high risk" offenders.

There were, however, some serious obstacles to Miller's plan. In Massachusetts, Miller had been Commissioner of the Department of Youth Services with the authority "to establish necessary facilities for detention, diagnosis, treatment, and training of its charges, including post-release care," with full control of juvenile institutions, with authority to place juveniles referred by the court, and with a departmental budget and staff (Rutherford, 1974). In Pennsylvania, he had none of this authority and, initially, none of these resources.

In late March of 1975, the Secretary and Deputy Secretary of the Department of Public Welfare accompanied Miller on a tour of the Camp Hill facility. Apparently, they were distressed by what they saw because the secretary promised funds to improve conditions while an effort to remove all juveniles from the facility was being mounted.

On April 2, 1975, a 16 year old Camp Hill inmate committed suicide by hanging himself in his cell. Other inmates maintained that he had been homosexually raped by a group of boys earlier in the day. They also claimed that there were no institutional staff members present on the cell block when he hanged himself. This youth had been sent to a county detention center after his parents referred him to the court for marijuana use. He ran away from that facility and stole a car in the process. The judge then sent him to Camp Hill. Except for the auto theft and runaway after his initial detention, he apparently had not had previous contact with the police or courts. CBS's "Sixty Minutes" came in to do a feature story on the suicide and on conditions in the institution. This event did much to strengthen the argument for removing juveniles from this facility.

In early April, the Department of Public Welfare began to negotiate the initial contracts to get the project underway. Shortly thereafter, an application for LEAA funding was prepared and submitted. The LEAA proposal, using data from December 1974, characterized the Camp Hill population in the following manner:

> While 185 youth are committed for offenses which could in some way be classed as crimes against persons, including one for homicide, 48 for armed robbery and 23 for rape (the remaining charges being less certain as to the danger involved to others), no less than 207 (or 52.7%) have been committed for offenses which do not involve danger to others, such as property offenses, and surely do not warrant incarceration in an adult prison. Furthermore, the fact that some youth sit in Camp Hill for charges such as "runaway" from juvenile correctional facilities" (to which the youth may have been committed for a status offense), "nonpayment of fines," "incorrigibility" (a status offense), and "malicious mischief to gravestones" are compelling reasons to develop alternatives with the utmost speed.

On April 15, the attorney general was persuaded to sign a letter to the juvenile court judges announcing that Camp Hill would be closed to new juvenile referrals as of August 15, 1975. In mid-May the Center for Community Alternatives, a private, nonprofit organization, was created to administer the removal of juveniles from Camp Hill and to develop community placements (for Camp Hill youngsters and for other "high-risk offenders" referred by the courts).

In mid-June the Center for Community Alternatives assigned three staff members to work inside the Camp Hill facility. These workers were to carry out the interim program for which the Secretary of Public Welfare had promised financial support.

Recreational programs, trips outside of the institution, visits from family and "community" groups (on buses provided by the project), a phone system on which inmates could call their families, and entertainment programs were planned. Staff were to get to know the kids so that they could be of assistance in facilitating the development of release plans. The assumption that this group would also perform an "advocacy" function seems to have been held by everyone associated with the project. It was never clear, however, what form such advocacy was to take, or on what authority it was believed to rest.

Few of the planned activities ever got off the ground. Some of this failure must be attributed to the fact that the funds promised by the Department of Public Welfare did not become available until the fall. In addition, these newly proposed activities threatened to be quite disruptive of institutional routine and were therefore opposed by the institutional staff, despite the superintendent's general support for the project. And finally, there was considerable confusion and growing disagreement within the project (both within and outside of the institution) regarding both project priorities and intervention techniques. Although six more staff members were assigned to the institution in late July, the function of this group remained unclear until at least mid-August.

The Center for Community Alternatives divided the state into four regions corresponding to the Department of Public Welfare's regionalization format. During June the four regional directors were hired. By August 1, the regional officers were said to be staffed and operative. Regional personnel were to be responsible for securing alternative placement options, the majority of which were expected to be developed through purchase of service contracts with local service vendors. According to the proposal, a team of "youth development specialists" was to formalize release plans for the Camp Hill youngsters, based on the alternative resources available and the individual's personal needs and interests. Finally, a "court liaison officer" was to negotiate the release of institutionalized youngsters with the committing judge. In practice, the "youth development specialist" positions were never operationalized;

consequently, the responsibility to develop plans fell primarily to the "court liaison officer."

Alternative placements were slow to develop. An Outward Bound program became operative in York County in August. Considerable time elapsed before other programs got off the ground. It was well into fall before staff from the southeast region visited Camp Hill to interview inmates for the purpose of developing release plans and it was winter before appreciable numbers of youngsters from this region left the institution on plans developed by the Center for Community Alternatives staff.

In an interview with Ken Lear of the Philadelphia *Tribune* on June 28, 1975, Miller had said, "There are about 400 juveniles at Camp Hill and they will all be out of there by August 15th ... and we want to have all the youths at the Youth Development Center out in less than a year." It is, of course, possible that Miller's statement was intended more to generate enthusiasm and support for project activities than to accurately set project timetables. It is clear, however, that virtually every step in the project's development took longer than anyone had initially anticipated. As August 15 approached, it became increasingly clear that, except for juveniles leaving at the normal rate of release, little was happening. Between the time of the attorney general's letter of April 15 and the August 15 target date, the state's juvenile court judges had continued to commit kids to Camp Hill.

Because the kids were not being moved by the regional staff, and because the "interim program" was foundering, the role of the nine staff members in Camp Hill was redefined so that they became primarily responsible for developing release plans. In fact, under the leadership of one member of the staff who was later to become the director of the "Camp Hill Unit" within the institution, the "interim program" staff had already been moving in this direction well before the official decision to do so.

Sole authority for release of juveniles at Camp Hill rested with the committing judge. Historically, judges had, in almost all instances, released juveniles on the dates recommended by the institution. Although juveniles came from the court *without* a fixed release date (virtually all had an indeterminate to three year sentence), the institutional "diagnostic clinic" set a date within the first three months of the juvenile's arrival at the institution. While this date was adjusted downward or upward slightly according to the staff's assessment of the juvenile's adjustment, this date rather than the indeterminate to three year sentence became the operational sentence against which the Camp Hill project had to negotiate. When an individual's release date approached, the institutional counselor and the juvenile shared in the task of developing an "acceptable" plan. The plan included living arrangements (usually with the family), a job or plans to return to school, and occasionally other supportive services. As staff of the Camp Hill Unit became involved in the release procedure, their role became one of facilitating this process. In this context, they assumed an advocacy role, negotiating with counselors, making contacts in the juvenile's home community (including family, potential employers, the court, etc.), writing release plans, and accumulating arguments supportive of these plans. On August 15, 1975, there had been 357 juveniles in Camp Hill; on June 15, 1976, there were 55; on September 15, 1976, there were 9; on March 15, 1977, there were 2. The following three sections of this paper will discuss the methodology employed in this analysis, the characteristics of the juvenile population at Camp Hill, and the relationship of the task of removing juveniles from Camp Hill to the larger reform goals of Miller and the Center for Community Alternatives.

Before proceeding, however, the reader is offered a cautionary note. While there is a tendency to treat this process as a "deinstitutionalization" effort and to think in terms of closing Camp Hill, such terms must be avoided if the dynamics of the project are to be understood. Camp Hill was officially an adult institution and as juveniles were removed, adults came in to replace them. Therefore, no institutional jobs were at stake and the continued existence of the institution was never threatened. In fact, the existence of a juvenile and an adult population, with the requirement that they be kept separate, imposed real problems for the administration. While many institutional staff were ideologically opposed to the project and while many appear to have felt threatened, one could reasonably argue that institutional interests were best served by converting to an exclusively adult facility. This fact does much to explain both the superintendent's supportive stance toward the project and the absence of opposition from the employee's union. The impact of this situation will be considered in the final section.

METHODOLOGY

Nothing will cool the ardor of an enthusiastic researcher more than exposure to Pennsylvania's record-keeping systems for juvenile offenders. A number of state agencies maintain independent and overlapping records, as do the county governments involved. The result is that any systematic study of juvenile offenders must begin from the ground up. In preparing this paper, we obtained information on the subject population from institutional records and from project files. We quickly discovered that the quality of record keeping in the juvenile courts and at the state-run facility was poor. Consequently, there is some missing information on every characteristic studied.

Our knowledge of the project was enhanced considerably by our ongoing relationships with most of the principals involved. Both of the authors became involved in data collection efforts early in the development of the project and in that capacity had ongoing contacts with project administrators and workers from the moment Dr. Miller first arrived in the state. One of the authors had previously worked on a research project in the institution and consequently was familiar with the institution's history and practices regarding the juvenile population.

We were able to obtain complete information on 55 of the Camp Hill youngsters, who were personally interviewed during the months of May and June 1976. This group consisted of all youth remaining in the facility on those dates. In addition to questions bearing upon demographic data, we asked the youth a number of open-ended questions about the role played by the

Camp Hill project staff in the institution, their attitudes toward both the project and the institution, and related issues.

Given the difficulties emanating from the poor quality of existing records, gaps in the data on the Camp Hill youth were to be expected. Despite these problems, however, it is essential that we attempt to present the existing data, such as it is, as the project is no more, the kids are out of Camp Hill, and no one has yet attempted to analyze this significant change.

In the following paragraphs we will focus on several concerns we consider to be of central importance in an analysis of the Camp Hill project. While other factors may also be of interest, our analysis has pinpointed these issues as critical to an understanding of what has occurred.

CHARACTERISTICS OF THE CAMP HILL JUVENILE POPULATION

County of Commitment

There was considerable variation from county to county with regard to commitments to the Camp Hill facility. Among Pennsylvania's 67 counties, 18 (generally rural counties with small populations) had not committed any youth to Camp Hill during the period under study, and another 39 sent from one to six juveniles there. We classified the latter counties as "low commitment" areas; together they accounted for 24% of all juveniles housed at the facility.

A total of seven counties were classified as having "medium commitment" rates. Their referrals ranged from seven to 15 youth; together they accounted for 22% of the youth population at Camp Hill.

The remaining three counties (accounting for 30% of the state's population) were classified as "high commitment" areas; together they accounted for 54% of all Camp Hill youth. These three high commitment counties include Allegheny (located in the western region of the state and containing the city of Pittsburgh), Dauphin (located in the central region of the state and containing the state capital of Harrisburg), and Philadelphia (located in the southeastern region of the state and containing the city of Philadelphia). In some instances, the juveniles sent to Camp Hill from these locations were the more serious offenders who had committed violent acts or major property crimes, and many had extensive records of such offenses. There were exceptions however.

We noted that one high commitment county presented an unexpected number of referrals to Camp Hill. Dauphin County, the site of the state capital, referred 54 of the 357 youngsters (15%, while the county contains fewer than 2% of the state's population). Allegheny County, with a population that is more than seven times larger, referred 53 youngsters (15%), and Philadelphia (almost nine times larger) referred 86 juveniles (24%).

Unless one could argue convincingly that the juvenile "crime problem" is more severe in Dauphin County than in the other high commitment areas, these youths must be seen as considerably overrepresented in the Camp Hill juvenile population. One explanation may be that some local judges view this institution as "their own," since the facility is located within five miles of the city of Harrisburg. Thus, they may argue that referral to this facility is more desirable than sending a youngster to one of the Youth Development Centers located considerable distances from the region and consequently out of reach of the youths' families. A less benign interpretation would suggest that, regardless of the court's motives for doing so, many Dauphin County youths were inappropriately placed in a facility which was both more restrictive and more punitive than other dispositional alternatives. Moreover, there is persuasive evidence that the latter interpretation may be correct, for one of the three Dauphin County judges committed 30 juveniles to Camp Hill, *the second highest commitment rate of any juvenile judge in the entire state,* and nearly twice as high as the third highest, a Philadelphia judge who had committed 17 youths to the facility.

A second example of judicial inconsistency is provided by an Allegheny County judge who was personally responsible for committing 33 juveniles to Camp Hill during the study period; *his referrals account for 9% of the entire juvenile population at that institution!* The next highest commitment rate for an Allegheny County judge was 14. This same judge had a rate of commitment more than twice that of any other judge in his county, leading us to conclude that his sentencing practices were considerably at odds with those of his colleagues, unless one could assume an unequal distribution of cases with this judge seeing more youngsters, and more serious offenders, than his fellows. We know that this judge was one of the most outspoken critics of the Camp Hill project from its inception until its demise, and project workers reported that he had refused, in most instances, to cooperate with their efforts. Of the 11 youths still in the institution on September 15, 1976, five were committed by this judge.

The wards of the three high commitment counties were also kept in the prison for longer terms than youths from the medium and low commitment counties. The high commitment counties were responsible for 54% of the total juvenile population at the institution, yet these youths accounted for only 36% of the one to six month sentences and 39% of the seven to 12 month sentences (we refer to these sentences as "short commitments"). Thus, these counties were underrepresented in the short-term sentence categories. Among those serving longer sentences, the same counties accounted for 65% of the 13 to 18 month sentences, 79% of the 19 to 24 month sentences, and 75% of all sentences in excess of 24 months.

Since the majority of black youths came from these counties, it may be that racial inequities with regard to time served account for much of this difference. This matter will be considered in the following section. It is also possible that youths from the high commitment counties received longer sentences because the offenses for which they had been committed were more serious. Data relating time served to commitment offense was examined. Offense types were categorized into crimes against the person (forcible rape, assault robbery, etc.), crimes against property (burglary, larceny, auto theft, etc.), revocation of parole or probation or institutional runaway, and, finally, miscellaneous offenses. When we examined the length of time served by commitment offense the expected relationship between "person" crimes and longer sentences was not always found. For example, among the population of 142 "person" offenders, 57 (40%) served short sentences of one to 12 months, while 85 (60%) served sentences of more than one year. Among the 136 property offenders, 75 (55%) served one to 12 month sentences and 61 (45%) served sentences of more than one year. Given these figures, it is apparent that although "person" offenders generally served longer sentences, a sizable group did not; similarly, among property offenders a large number of youths also received the harsher penalties. Thus, the nature of the offense alone is not adequate to explain the variation in time served.

Finally, it is conceivable that the demeanor of urban youths at the institution's "diagnostic clinic" was such that they were given longer "sentences" by the clinic staff and/or that the subsequent behavior of urban youths (the majority of whom were black) was seen by the predominantly white nonurban staff as sufficiently inappropriate as to warrant lengthier periods of confinement.

Our understanding of the dynamics and conditions in the county juvenile courts is insufficient to warrant further analysis. It is clear, however, that substantial discrepancies exist among counties in their utilization of the Camp Hill facility. Regional or rural/urban differences in the extent or severity of delinquent misbehavior appear to be insufficient explanations of the phenomena. One also encounters different commitment rates among judges, both across and within jurisdictions, which suggest the existence of dramatically differing opinions regarding the appropriate utilization of Camp Hill. When one considers that committing offense bears no strong relationship to time served, the disproportionately lengthy sentences received by youths from "high commitment" counties is also disconcerting. While the causes of these discrepancies may be unclear, the data certainly suggest that equity and rationality are not the guiding principles by which commitment decisions are made.

Race

Many have argued that judges in Pennsylvania discriminate against blacks in terms of numbers of commitments, and in length of time served for those so committed. The judges often argue that such figures reflect a disproportionate involvement by blacks in youthful criminal activities, and especially in serious delinquencies. It is essential to consider the racial issue since it was evident that blacks were considerably overrepresented in the Camp Hill population. Of the 357 youngsters, 202 (57%) were black. (The black population of Pennsylvania constitutes 9% of the total.)

As is true in much of the North, Pennsylvania's black population is located predominantly within the large metropolitan centers of the state. Given this fact, one would not expect to find a sizable number of black commitments to Camp Hill from the state's primarily rural counties. In looking at the county commitment figures we find support for this notion, as 48 counties (72% of the total) had no black commitments among the 59 youths they sent to Camp Hill. On the other hand, the three urbanized high commitment counties accounted for 160 *or 79% of all black commitments to the facility.* While 76% (41 of 54) of the Dauphin County juveniles were black, only 12% of the Dauphin County population is black. While 66% (35 of 53) of Allegheny County juveniles were black, only 9% of the county population is black. And while *98% (84 of 86) of the Philadelphia County juveniles were black* only 34% of the county population is black. (In an earlier study, Wolfgang et al., 1972, also noted considerable discrimination in the Philadelphia court system's dealings with blacks.)

An examination of the relationship between race and time served provides the most telling evidence of racial inequity. Table 1 presents this data. If one recalls that there is no strong relationship between time served and severity of offense, one finds support for the contention that blacks are treated more punitively than are their white counterparts. The data show that blacks serve inordinately long sentences when contrasted with whites, as 61% of blacks as opposed to 36% of whites serve terms of more than one year.

Table 1

	Race	
Time Served	White	Black
1-6 months	76	24
7-12 months	52.2	47.7
13-18 months	37.2	62.8
19-24 months	11.6	86.0
25+ months	25.0	68.8

In reviewing the rates of commitments for blacks and whites from the high commitment counties, it was apparent that the former were being discriminated against *by some judges in some counties*. Again, it is possible that the lengthy sentences served by most blacks was a product of institutional racism, as the staff at the facility was actually responsible in most instances for setting the release dates of juveniles housed there. These data, like the data on county of commitment, raise serious doubts regarding the equity of the facility and its use.

Commitment Offense and Arrest History

Pennsylvania's juvenile court judges often argue that they only use the Camp Hill facility for the most intractable youth appearing before them, and that commitment to this institution is the only answer for dealing with the state's toughest delinquents. Given these claims, we felt it appropriate to look closely at the arrest records of the youth incarcerated in that facility to determine if they were in fact serious offenders. In looking at the original commitment offenses for the Camp Hill juvenile population, we found that 142 (40%) were referred for crimes against the person (with specific offenses ranging from petty gang fights to murder and everything in between), 136 (39%) for property offenses (such as auto theft, burglary, and larceny), 54 (15%) were runaways from YDC placements or had had their probation or parole revoked, and 19 (5%) had been placed in the prison for a variety of other offenses.

Following this preliminary breakdown we looked at each youth's arrest history and arrived at the figures presented in Table 2. At one end of the continuum, 17 youths had experienced no prior arrests. Although they were few in

Table 2

Prior Arrests	N	%
None	17	5.7
1-2	72	24.0
3-5	117	39.0
6-10	65	21.7
11+	29	9.6
Total	300	100.0

number, the fact that these youths were sent to Camp Hill rather than to a YDC facility or some other correctional placement is puzzling for their specific commitment offenses do not indicate that they were especially serious offenders or that they could not have been handled adequately in a considerably less secure setting. On the other extreme, we find 29 youths who had accumulated more than 11 arrests each. The majority of the Camp Hill population fell between these two extremes. A total of 94 of the youths had been arrested six or more times, and while this group unquestionably constituted the "hard core offender" category, they comprised only 31% of all the youth sent there. (The discrepancy between the number and the percentage figure is explained by numerous instances of missing arrest data in institutional files.) Thus, there is some question whether the judge's contention was accurate, for 30% of the youths had two or fewer prior arrests at the time of their Camp Hill commitments.

Another concern was whether the Camp Hill youth had been tried in less secure placements before being sent to the maximum security facility, as the judges had claimed. Again we found a wide range of practices, as 63 of the youths had no previous institutional commitments, while 101 had one, 72 had two, 53 had three, 25 had four, five had five, and six had six. Twenty percent of those detained in Camp Hill had been sent to no other placement. This latter finding does not support the contention of those who claimed that Camp Hill was used only as a last resort after youngsters had first been tried in other placements.

In conclusion, we have noted considerable variation in judicial behavior with regard to Camp Hill commitments. In many instances, Camp Hill *is not* used solely for serious juvenile offenders with long criminal records, for we discovered a large number of youths in the facility who had few or no previous arrests. We also found that in many instances Camp Hill *is not* used only after other less secure institutional placements have been tried, as 20% of the population had had no prior commitments. This is not to suggest that all or even many of Pennsylvania's juvenile judges have been indiscriminate in their use of the institution. It does suggest, however, that at least *some judges appear to have been using that facility inappropriately,* and that such practices are likely to have produced deleterious consequences for the first offender or the juvenile experiencing his first institutional stay.

CONCLUSIONS

Objections to Camp Hill

Miller and his followers had argued that because of the presence of both a juvenile and an adult population in Camp Hill, the spirit and probably the letter of the law, as established in Pennsylvania's Juvenile Act, was being violated. Enforced idleness, the dearth of educational, vocational, and recreational opportunities for juveniles occasioned by the institution's attempts to segregate the juvenile population from contact with adults strengthened the argument.

Data presented in the previous section suggest that: (1) there were dramatic inconsistencies in utilization of Camp Hill both among counties and even among judges within the same counties, (2) juveniles at Camp Hill were not, in all instances, there because they had committed serious offenses, because they had unsuccessfully been tried in less secure institutions, or because they had lengthy arrest histories, (3) blacks were significantly overrepresented in the population (juvenile court practices) and were required to serve disproportionately longer sentences in the institution (primarily institutional practices).

The authors found no evidence to support the argument that Camp Hill was a necessary or even useful component of the state's juvenile justice system. We would conclude, with Miller, that both the court's use of the facility and practices within the institution were such as to repudiate any claim that the institution served any of the helping or rehabilitative functions demanded by juvenile justice philosophy. Given the obvious inappropriateness of such a facility, we are only surprised that it took a Jerry Miller and over a year of intense controversy to discontinue its use.

Resistance to Change

Both Miller and the Center for Community Alternatives staff anticipated considerable resistance from both the juvenile courts and the institutional staff at Camp Hill. In fact, resistance from these sources was never as intense or efficient as many had expected. Many judges were suspicious at first, several were openly hostile throughout the course of the project; but many more were more cooperative than had been anticipated. Unlike the Massachusetts judges, Pennsylvania juvenile courts had the full power to place youths, to transfer them, and to release them. Except for removing Camp Hill as a dispositional option, the project was not really a threat to the court's authority. Had it been otherwise, the massive and organized resistance expected from the courts would probably have materialized. To the extent that they opposed Miller and his people, the juvenile court judges appear to have been responding more to what they feared *might* happen than to what was actually taking place.

Except for the Camp Hill superintendent, institutional staff were initially quite hostile to the Camp Hill project. Even here, however, resistance never reached the proportions which had been anticipated earlier. As more and more youths were moved, it became increasingly apparent that the institution and institutional jobs were not really threatened. While only a few institutional staff were ever genuinely helpful to the project, their efforts to actively subvert project activities had ceased by mid-winter. As with the judges, had vested institutional interests really been threatened, the relationship may well have been very different.

Alternative Placements

The principle failure of project planning appears to have been their inability to anticipate the difficulty in finding acceptable individuals and organizations with whom to contract for alternative services. The amount of time and staff effort required to identify service providers, negotiate contracts, satisfy housing code standards, fight zoning battles, and get a prospective placement to the point at which it could accept clients was seriously underestimated.

Not surprisingly, the service providers often insisted on retaining control over who was to be placed within their facility. They often saw direct referrals from the courts as more attractive clients than the youth in Camp Hill. The Camp Hill project had expected to negotiate with the juvenile court judges; they were not prepared, however, to negotiate with their own service providers. This was a form of resistance that was never really anticipated and, consequently, the project was continually being caught off guard by these developments.

The Project

Although there at first appeared to be universal support among the project staff for project goals, a heated conflict soon developed regarding project priorities. One group was primarily concerned with establishing viable alternative programs to which youngsters could be referred; the other group wanted to get the kids out of Camp Hill immediately and any placement was good enough. The latter group saw in institutionalization the ultimate unforgivable evil; anything else was better than that. Every day that a kid spent at Camp Hill represented a failure of the project. They could not tolerate the delays associated with setting up community programs, contracting, etc. This group's most aggressive spokesman, an individual who had been with Miller in Massachusetts and Illinois, characterized the split as the "kid people versus the bureaucrats."

The other side (except perhaps for the regional staff) was every bit as committed to deinstitutionalization as were the "kid people." Their perspective, however, was different. They reasoned that, whereas Miller had had authority to move juveniles into the community in Massachusetts, no such power base existed here; whereas Miller had press, public, and political support in Massachusetts, no such support existed here. They feared that a number of high visibility failures in questionable placements could lead to massive political and institutional resistance. In the absence of real authority such resistance would, they reasoned, prove fatal. They also wanted to get the kids out of Camp Hill, but they wanted to move them to attractive community placements. They reasoned that since Camp Hill was only the first step in a larger effort at system reform, the removal of Camp Hill youth had to be accomplished in a manner which set the groundwork for further system change. They would have argued that the "kid people" in their singular attention to getting the kids out immediately and at any cost had lost sight of the project's larger system objectives. (The "kid people" would obviously have disagreed.)

The establishment of regional offices also led to internal problems. None of the regional staff had been involved in early project activities. They do not appear to have shared the anti-institutional, anti-court, pro-youth ideology of Miller and the early project staff. Their distance from the central offices and the youth in Camp Hill combined with their daily contact with local court and justice officials would appear to have generated substantially different organizational priorities at the local level than those at the central offices. The "bureaucrats" at the central offices were impatient with the regional staff; the "kid people" were furious.

Like many of the service providers, a number of staff in the regional offices seem to have perceived the Camp Hill youngsters as less attractive clients than were juveniles appearing before the court. According to project plans, only court referrals of youth who would have been sent to Camp Hill were to be accepted. It appears, however, that the courts were referring, and the regions were accepting, youth who would not have been institutionalized at all (either at Camp Hill or at Youth Development Centers) had the project not existed. Central office staff wanted to handle those cases which the juvenile courts considered to be the most serious and to deal with them using the "least restrictive alternative." The behavior of regional staff did much to undermine this top-down, "deep-end" strategy. Since resources were limited, internal conflicts were intensified.

Regional staff rarely visited the Camp Hill facility. What contact they had with these youngsters was through the staff working at the prison. While southeast regional staff came to the institution and interviewed all juveniles from their region, they took a lengthy period of time before submitting plans to the court. Unlike the other regions, the southeast opted to work through existing agencies (primarily OIC) rather than to identify completely new service resources. It is difficult to determine whether their slowness to act was a function of the established agencies' unwillingness to move quickly to deal with these youngsters, or whether it reflected the regional staff's own cautious attitudes. Whatever the cause, the southeastern region was by far the slowest to move kids, even though they experienced little resistance from the Philadelphia courts. (Few plans were rejected by judges from this region; probably none were rejected from December 1975 on.) This is particularly ironic, since the project had gone to great lengths to employ an almost exclusively minority staff in the southeast region to insure effective and equitable treatment to this predominantly black inmate population.

Success or Failure

As mentioned earlier, the removal of juveniles from Camp Hill was seen as the initial step in a sweeping deinstitutionalization movement. If the juveniles at Camp Hill could be returned to the community without major problems, the logic of the continued commitment of juveniles to other Pennsylvania institutions would be seriously undermined. Success at Camp Hill was expected to lead to further deinstitutionalization. Despite continued efforts by Miller, now Commissioner of Children and Youth in the Department of Public Welfare, and a handful of supporters, it does not appear that other institutions will be closed to juveniles in the near future. The Center for

Community Alternatives ceased to exist as of June 30, 1976. All but two juveniles were out of Camp Hill as of March 15, 1977. The alternative programs funded by the center are currently being funded by the Department of Public Welfare. These facilities continue to accept referrals from the courts. On May 25, 1976, a juvenile court judge attempted to commit a juvenile to Camp Hill challenging the attorney general's ruling. The youth was at the institution for a few days until a superior court ruling removed him pending a final decision of the issue. The final decision has yet to be reached. It appears, however, that the attorney general's ruling will stand and that Camp Hill will have been successfully closed to juvenile referrals.

Even the authors cannot agree on whether or not the project was a success or a failure. Both are supportive of the reform goals of the project; both are disappointed that change with respect to the utilization of Camp Hill has not resulted in substantive change *throughout* the state's juvenile justice system.

Without the aggressive support of either the juvenile court or any branch of state government, without the authority to make decisions regarding the placement or movement of delinquent youth, and without widespread public support for project objectives, one might find it surprising that anything was accomplished. The absence of genuine power or authority often led project staff to choose between high-risk decisions or inactivity. In retrospect, many of these decisions may be seen by some as irresponsible. Certainly the hostile evaluator could find sufficient material to mount a convincing argument (and the sympathetic evaluator will develop an equally impressive case). The authors hold the opinion that evaluation at the policy level would be difficult; that evaluation at the operational level would be impossible. The intense debate regarding juvenile justice deinstitutionalization centers around political rather than programmatic or operational questions. The purpose of this paper is to present a brief account of the history of the Camp Hill project, not to pass judgment on its outcome.

REFERENCES

RUTHERFORD, A. (1974). The dissolution of the training schools in Massachusetts. Columbus: Academy for Contemporary Problems.

WOLFGANG, M., FIGLIO, R., and SELLIN, T. (1972). Delinquency In a birth cohort. Chicago: University of Chicago Press.

ABOUT THE AUTHORS

ROY L. AUSTIN received his Ph.D. in Sociology from the University of Washington in 1973. He is currently Assistant Professor of Sociology at the Pennsylvania State University.

RICHARD A. BALL, currently Professor of Sociology at West Virginia University, received his Ph.D. in Sociology from Ohio State University in 1965.

BRUCE BULLINGTON, Ph.D., is currently Associate Professor, Division of Community Development, College of Human Development, Pennsylvania State University.

SUSAN K. DATESMAN, a Ph.D. candidate at the University of Delaware, is currently Research Coordinator for the Evaluation of Status Offender Project, University of Delaware.

TERENCE DUNGWORTH, Ph.D., is currently affiliated with the Institute for Law and Social Research, Washington, D.C., and the School of Criminal Justice, Michigan State University.

THEODORE N. FERDINAND, Professor of Sociology at Northern Illinois University, received his Ph.D. in 1961 from the University of Michigan. He is the author of *Typologies of Delinquency* (1966), *Juvenile Delinquency* (1975), as well as numerous journal articles.

CURT T. GRIFFITHS received his Ph.D. in 1977 from the University of Montana. He is currently Assistant Professor of Criminology, Simon Fraser University.

THOMAS D. McDONALD is an Associate Professor in Sociology/Anthropology and Coordinator of the Criminal Justice System Program at North Dakota State University.

FRANK R. SCARPITTI, Ph.D., is currently Professor of Sociology and Chairman of the Department of Sociology at the University of Delaware.

ELDON C. SCHRINER is Chairman of the Department of Sociology/Anthropology and Associate Director of the Center for Social Research at North Dakota State University.

JAMES T. SPROWLS is affiliated with the Division of Community Development at the Pennsylvania State University. His Ph.D. training is in Community Systems Planning and Development.

JERI J. THILMONY is currently a lecturer in the Department of Sociology/Anthropology at North Dakota State University and a Juvenile Probation Officer with Clay County Family Court Services of Minnesota.

L. THOMAS WINFREE, Jr., Assistant Professor in the Department of Sociology and Anthropology, East Texas State University, received his Ph.D. in 1976 from the University of Montana.